THE REAL MANHUNTER CASEBOOK

THE REAL MANHUNTER CASEBOOK

COLIN SUTTON

REVELATION FILMS

First published in Great Britain in 2025 by Revelation Films

Paperback ISBN 978-1-0683938-1-5
eBook ISBN 978-1-0683938-0-8

Revelation Films
7 Ridgmount Street
London, WC1E 7AE

www.revelationfilms.co.uk

CONTENTS

PROLOGUE

I grew up in a police family. My dad was in the job, he was a PC in Edmonton, north London, and then went to traffic. I grew up, I suppose, with him and his mates from work.

I'm only child and I was taken along with mum and dad quite often. My mum insisted, so I kind of knew all of his colleagues, I'm still in touch with those who are still alive. And so I suppose I was sort of immersed in that kind of police family and socialising from quite a young age.

It does have an impact on you. My dad was a copper and it really does have an influence on you, the way you act, social skills and more. I found it when I joined the job, there were still people in the job that were serving with my dad. It was part of my life.

I was born and grew up in Enfield, north London on the poor side of the A10. Enfield is divided by that road out of London, the Great Cambridge Road, the A10. If you live one side it was a bit grubby, there used to be industry and all sorts of things down to Brimsdown where I lived. It's all changed very much now.

My dad was a PC in the Met and my mum had a few jobs and was a clerk in the solicitor's office and gradually worked her way through doing various things. She became a conveyancer, and then finally she became an expert in liquor licensing by the time she retired in her late 60s. She'd probably worked for at least one out of three supermarkets throughout the country, they had contracts to do the licensing work with the big supermarket chains and the Co-op.

Mum and dad were pretty humble, ordinary working class Londoners. We spent the first 10 years of my life living with my mum's parents in Enfield. She was insistent that she didn't want to go to a police house or police flat because she'd rather save up so that they could buy their own house. And it wasn't until I was 10 that they achieved that - and we only moved literally 600 yards away.

After school, I went to do law at university in Leeds. But by that time I'd been working for my mum's solicitor's firm as a clerk. I went to court, assisting the barrister, taking the papers along while I was in the sixth form and while I was at university. And I'd decided that I didn't want to be part of this idea of helping people to get away with things.

I'd been involved in the culture and community of the police from childhood, but I felt a little bit embarrassed whenever people said: "Oh, you're going to be a policeman like your dad." Because in my heart I knew I would be but thought it was expected that I wouldn't. Mum especially wasn't very keen on the idea, so I never really let on.

I think I was too immature to go away to university. I found it quite hard going up to Leeds, I did all right academically, I always have done, but I decided there was no point in it. I wanted to join the police and I didn't want to delay that for a degree which I didn't need. It was unusual, at the time, going into policing with A-levels and having dropped out of university, but I decided it was what I really wanted. So I applied to the Met while I was at university at Leeds.

What I didn't know was, of course you have to give your home address, not university address. And I didn't know they acknowledged your application with a postcard. Of course, the postcard turned up at home, mum and dad saw it, and the next thing I know they were banging on the door of my university flat having driven 200 miles up the M1 to ask: "What's all this about?"

We went out and had a Berni Inn steak and talked about it. And I told them that I had thought about it and it's what I wanted to do and I was going to do it. And from that moment on, they were just behind me and they still are. They have been incredibly supportive of me for all of my life.

I did a year and a term at Leeds but dropped out from university in 1980. (I did eventually get my law degree, courtesy of good fortune in the Met.)

I went for my Met recruitment interview, in November, 1980. One of my friends had applied just before me and he'd got a date to start in February 1981. So I was expecting it'd be Easter-time, maybe April, that I'd go if I got selected.

I was successful in my application and somebody, I don't know who this man was to this day, but somebody broke his leg and told the Met: “Sorry, I'm going to have to delay my joining because I can’t start, I've broken my leg, I'm not fit enough to join.” He was due to join on January 5, 1981, but he told them on December 23 and the recruiting department didn’t want to have an empty slot on the course but thought that with the Christmas post and holidays it would be hard to fill the place at such short notice.

Meanwhile, in the way these funny things happen and stars align, my dad was working at traffic control at Scotland Yard at the time; the central command complex for traffic police. Dad being dad, he was posted there because he'd given two fingers to the Chief Superintendent about something and had been sent there as a punishment posting for a year.

As the recruitment officers were literally looking through applications, trying to find a recruit to fill this spare place in January one of them realised: “Look, this one’s father works at traffic control so we can get the papers to him by hand and he can take them home for his son. Which means he could start earlier.” So they phoned me up at home and asked if I wanted to join in January, of course I was absolutely delighted, it meant my whole application from form to attestation took less than 10 weeks.

But that stroke of luck did more than move me forward a few months. It ended up making a real difference as to how my career would progress. I joined on January 5 1981. I went to training school, I enjoyed it, it was good fun. I trained at Wanstead, east London, rather than Hendon. We used to go to Hendon once a fortnight for drill and swimming. I found the academic work interesting and frankly pretty easy but threw myself into it and emerged with honours in the final exam and the book prize then given for the top student.

I got posted to Y District, which was the district that covered the boroughs of Enfield and Haringey. It was a kind of home posting, confirmed when I was told I would be going to Enfield as PC 504Y. But the father of my best friend intervened. Dave, who now lives in Austria, was never a policeman but his father Peter was Chief Superintendent at Tottenham and I knew him really well. Dave and I have been mates since we were 10 years old and we'd been on holiday with each other's family, and had generally spent most of our late childhood in each other's houses.

Peter intercepted my posting. He told me I wouldn't learn anything because in those days Enfield was a bit quiet and a bit of a backwater. So I ended up at Tottenham. I had no real ambitions to be anything other than a really good street policeman, that's what I wanted to do, that's who I wanted to be. And it was a good place to do it. Peter was a great mentor for me and I was devastated when he died, far too young, in 2001.

At Tottenham, I later found out, there was a little bit of suspicion – they knew I'd given up university to go there and I had A-levels, I'd been to a decent school and all that. It was a little bit unusual, but I mucked in and did what I could. On my first day, at 2pm on a Thursday, I paraded at Tottenham. By ten past two I was at the Coroner's Court and mortuary at Hornsey, reporting a sudden death case. And by four o'clock I was walking around Broadwater Farm. I was thinking: "What the hell? What have I done?"

It was only six miles down the road from where I had grown up but the difference was like night and day. I realise looking back that I'd had quite a cosseted life in Enfield and at school. Things out in the big wide world were very different. Broadwater Farm was challenging to police, even in the early eighties, four years before the riot.

I had no real ambitions to be anything other than a really good street policeman. That's what I wanted to do. That's what I wanted to be. It was a great place to learn how to do it. I'm still friends with people there and did my best to get involved.

I went to training once a month, did an exam once a month and did my final probation exam in September 1982. I was coming up to two years in January 1983 and after the exam, which I passed with 96 per cent, I was called in to see the Chief Superintendent who had replaced Peter. He said: "Right, you've passed that very well, how do you feel about taking the sergeant's exam?"

I said: "I will do one day, sir."

But one of the best bits of advice my dad gave me, which I passed on to my son when he joined the police, was never turn down any opportunity for training, you never know when it's going to be useful to you.

And the senior officer looked at me and he said: "No, I meant in January this year, which is your two-year anniversary."

They said they'd sign the paperwork if I wanted to do it, and as I had in any case been studying for the past few months it was a good time to do it. So I agreed.

And that's where January 5 comes into it, because the sergeant's exam then was always on the first Saturday in January. But that year, 1983, the first of January was a Saturday, so it was a bank holiday and they put the exam back the second Saturday, which was the eighth. The regulations were that you had to have a minimum of two years' service on the day of the exam – I had two years in on the fifth, so I made it by three days. If that bloke hadn't had broken his leg, then I'd have joined later. I couldn't have taken the exam at the point I did and who knows what then would have happened? It's just fate.

I went along to Ponders End police station to the promotion classes that had already been running for about six weeks and the Sergeant, Bob Barker – who I worked with as an inspector later, he's a very good guy – pulled me to one side and said: "You've got no chance, They're six weeks ahead of you. There's no point in you coming here." I understood his thinking but I was determined. You didn't have to attend classes to take the exam but every year virtually everyone who succeeded had done so.

All of which only really served to make me think: "Yes, I'm going to do it."

I saved all my leave up. My Inspector, the late Dave Stobbs, who was really very instrumental in preparing me to be a leader, organised for me to be the warden at the section house for a month. There was somebody sick and I was sitting there studying. I took about 10 days off in a row around Christmas, and I didn't do any studying on Boxing Day, or on Christmas Day, otherwise I didn't go out of the house. I sat there, cramming and cramming and cramming. I was even cramming in between the two papers that I did on the

Saturday of the exam, while sitting in my friend's car that had got us to Hendon.

Anyway, I passed. Not only that, but it was done competitively then. Results were published in order of score and I was 27th in the whole Met. They wanted 400 or so sergeants that year, but you couldn't be promoted even if you were in the top 400 until you had five years' service. And I only had two and a bit. "That's OK, I've got that," I thought, "that's in the bank, I can do something for the next few weeks and months and years."

Meanwhile, I was working as a community PC on Broadwater Farm Estate in Tottenham. All I did for four months was walk around the Farm and there's a limit to how many things you can have thrown at you before you get fed up with it. It was before the riots and it was really, really soul destroying. It was the only time of my service that I didn't like. The officer I was partnered up with and I used to walk the long way around from Tottenham nick to the Farm and try to lock somebody up on the way so we didn't have to go on there – our productivity was probably quite good.

As soon as the exam results came in, as they didn't have enough sergeants, anybody who passed was instantly deployed as an acting sergeant. So I left the Farm team and went back to a "relief" – a response team in today's cop-speak. But also, because I was in the top 100 for the sergeants exam, I had to go for the interviews for the special sergeant courses at Bramshill police college in Hampshire. And, remembering my dad's advice – "Don't ever give up anything that you get offered" – I went for the interviews and somehow got selected.

For the rest of 1983, I was an acting sergeant at Tottenham. At this time wasn't aware of any kind of antipathy or any kind of resentment among the other officers. I'd done my best to be busy and to work as hard as I could. I was 22 years old, I've got two years and three months' service, and I'm acting sergeant in Tottenham. I'm getting people like Winston Silcott wheeled in front of me for murder and things. It was a busy place and I kind of learned early on – and I'd talked about it with my dad – I think the worst thing I could have done was to pretend I knew more than I did. All I had to do was ask because I didn't think I was stupid, I could pick stuff up. I didn't need to be told twice – but I did need to be told.

And that kind of stood me in good stead, I think, as to how my career went because there were a few occasions when I found myself doing things that you wouldn't have thought I'd have been doing. And in some ways I think the best moments in life generally are through self-reflection when you are looking at yourself and thinking: "Gosh, am I really doing that?" When I stopped playing football and I started refereeing, the very first time I refereed a football match, I thought: "Is this really me doing this?" It doesn't have to be momentous things, but just stretching yourself and doing new things. I've had a lot of those moments since I retired too.

I started the Special Course on January 3 1984 and finished on December 18. Bramshill, for people who don't know – it was recently on the market again for about £11 million – is a Jacobean mansion in 273 acres of Hampshire countryside near the border with Berkshire. It didn't know at the time whether it was like Sandhurst due to the regimented nature of some aspects of police training, or whether it was a university due to the academia, it had trappings of both.

I was on the 22nd special course at Bramshill. You went there for a year, you did all sorts of studying, you did all sorts of practical things, and you came out and then spent a year back at your force as a sergeant. You took the inspector's exam while you were down at Bramshill, and as long as you passed and then did your year as a sergeant after, you were promoted to inspector.

I was 23 years old, I was the youngest on the course. There were 28 people on the course, all men, which is the first time the course had had no women. And I think about half of those – 12 or 14 – were from the Met.

I did my year at Bramshill, it was genuinely one of the best years of my life. I made friends there I will cherish for ever. I was told I would be going to Stoke Newington for my year as a sergeant, just next door to Tottenham, where I'd come from. But I thought I wasn't going to learn anything – it was just the same. It was the same people, just across the road. I pointed this out to the career development people and they offered me any division in Westminster or Kensington. I didn't fancy being a tour guide so I chose Paddington Green.

We had a huge team. I think we had seven sergeants and only one of them was over 35 and they were a great bunch of blokes, and I had a really good time there. I knew I was only going to be there for a year. We had the terrorist suite there, the security suite as it was known, which was all done on overtime. And you could earn a fortune doing that shift. It's funny how Special Branch always seemed to manage to bring somebody on bank holiday weekends, which we didn't complain about.

Some of my team had got more service than I had years on the planet and again, I had to fall back on thinking: "Look, I've got a couple of really experienced sergeants here. I need your help. I'm going to be leaning on you."

I knew though there would soon be another interruption to my police career. While I was on the special course at Bramshill, they came around and said: "Who hasn't got a degree?" There were just five of us and there were six places on offer to go and do a degree full time on what was known as a Bramshill Scholarship. "Fill in the form, and you've got it."

I asked to do German with linguistics but it was suggested the subject ought, broadly, to relate to policing. So I did another six months at Leyton, east London having been promoted to inspector and then I went to University College London, UCL. I was full-time for three years on full inspector's pay. And so I finally got my law degree.

I had to do all three years because my first year that I'd done at Leeds didn't count; it was too long afterwards. I was 26 when I went there and was at UCL until I was 29. I'd done so little policing that when it came to the holidays, I thought it was a bit daft. It was May, I'd finished and I wasn't back until the middle of September. I spoke to my contact back at the Met and told him that if I spent three years out, I didn't have that much experience to go back to, it'd be back starting again from scratch when I finished my degree.

So I did some police work during the holidays. It was very unusual. I even had a message from the Police Federation, it said: "We battled for years for people who were on these scholarships not to have to come back to work and you've done it."

And I just said: "Well, OK, I understand that for most people, but for me I think this is the right thing to do, so I'm going to do it."

I ended up going to Holloway, covering for the relief inspectors on their holidays. And it was brilliant. I don't know whether I'd grown up or whether I was more comfortable in my own skin about what I was doing, but I went there and I just took to it like a duck to water – the place the people, how we worked.

And as I was coming up to the end of my degree, the Chief Superintendent there said: "I've got a space I'm holding open for you if you want to come here permanently." In a heartbeat I said,: "Yeah, absolutely." So I started working there in 1987 and I was there for the next five years, on and off for the first two, but I then spent a long time on the relief at Holloway. They were just fantastic people, some of the best that I ever worked with.

I really enjoyed it there, but I had this thing in my head, I wanted to try some other things, become a detective and give that a go. I spoke to the DI at a Christmas do at Holloway and he said: "You haven't done the groundwork, Colin. You just carry on doing what you're doing, you'll be a bloody chief superintendent and you'll be fine. You like doing your public order and your football – we were doing Arsenal – and stuff. Be happy with that."

He said it in a nice way.

I'd got back on the high potential scheme – I ended up being on it twice. I'd been an inspector on paper since 1985, it was now 1992, I'd already done quite a big chunk of time in the rank. The Met then decided there would be no promotions to chief inspector for four years, there'd be a moratorium as they had too many senior officers. It was right, but I wasn't best pleased.

But the Met said to those like me on the high potential scheme: "While there are no promotions, we want to develop you? Is there anything you'd like to do?"

"Yeah, I'd like to be a DI please."

"Oh yeah, you can do that."

So I went to Islington as a DI, which is where The Real Manhunter starts…

I've been lucky enough to have two careers in my life – first as a police officer, then, after I retired from the Metropolitan Police, working in the media, first as a pundit, then working on true crime programmes.

Everything changed when I met Tony Carne and then Trevor Drane at Revelation Films. As soon as I met them, I knew that we had the same sort of approach to working on documentaries and true crime. Our aims were totally mutual, we had the same kind of beliefs too.

I'd done documentary programmes with other people, I'd made a lot of programmes with a lot of different companies, but this really was a chance to do it in a way that I thought it ought to be done.

That meant the right kind of tone and the right kind of focus, especially compared to what else was on TV then.

And that's why I committed to working with them and why I have remained committed to working with them. I like the way we do it, it's very different from the American headline-driven sensationalist way that was prevalent. As Trevor has said, when I started working on true crime, it was an industry that was "incredibly perpetrator focused and we want to move away from that", he was and is right, it was sensationalist, it was headline-driven and tabloid in style. I learned very quickly that I didn't want to be part of that.

But Tony and Trevor shared my vision. Revelation is an entrepreneur-driven production company whose founders call themselves "working class oiks"; they understood the importance of not turning these stories into tabloid fodder, that there were victims who had been wronged and that those victims had families who needed to be considered.

Now true crime programming has moved on and Revelation and myself, through The Real Manhunter, have helped move that along. I believe we've moved the dial a bit. I like to feel we've been instrumental in that.

As they'll say, other companies have now stolen that t-shirt and are trying to present themselves as movers and shakers in that area. They're trying to claim they are the leaders in being more detective and investigation-led, more sensitive towards the victims. But have a look at some of the programme and series titles they still use. They talk the talk but we walk the walk. We name our episodes after the victims – because they, we believe, are always the most important part of the story.

We've just finished shooting our fourth series. We started on cases I had been closely involved with, and have widened our scope beyond that to look at others as my cases have become exhausted.

And we always have the same motivation of looking at cases not from the notoriety of the killers and criminals, but from the perspective of the people who caught them and the people who suffered, the victims.

True crime holds a strange, macabre fascination for the public which when serving I didn't appreciate fully. I have taken The Real Manhunter on the road with a national theatre tour, it's just me, a projector and some slides, and I get to meet many of my viewers and readers which is a privilege, and gives me the opportunity to make my case for what I believe to be true.

I am not perfect, but I and my team did our best to serve the public and solve murder cases. The police generally too are not perfect, they reflect the society from which they are drawn to serve, but in my own small way, be it on TV, in print or on stage I try and relate what I did during my time as an officer and show the best of what I believe the police can be, to reassure people. There are lots of committed, dedicated and brave people out there who want to have your back. I think I am getting this message across, even if it is only one heart at a time.

CHAPTER 1
THE MURDER OF DUNCAN BONE

I went to Islington in October 1992, having been a uniformed inspector for seven years, three and a half of those spent at Holloway, the neighbouring division. Throughout that time, I'd had this dream almost, a sort of hankering, to be a detective. And because of the way my career path had gone with the accelerated promotion scheme, I hadn't had the chance to do it as a constable or sergeant.

I never thought I'd get the chance to be honest. The people at the top, in their infinite wisdom, decided that they had too many chiefs, and they said they weren't going to have any promotions to superintendent or chief inspector for some considerable time.

Having been an inspector for that long, I was sort of lined up to be doing that. All the people that had done the high potential scheme, including me, were still on that list. But the career management branch at Scotland Yard phoned up and said: "You know you're not going to be able to get promoted for the next year or three. [In fact it turned out to be four years.] Is there anything else you'd like to do that would sort of develop you in a different role without being promoted?"

"Well, I'd quite like to be a detective," I replied. They simply said I could do that. And that was it and that was how I came to be. So I went across to Islington. Where the Chief Superintendent was a bloke called Bill Sinclair and the DCI was called Eddie O'Connell. And they kind of knew me a bit and they gave me the opportunity to go across there and be a detective. I'd not done any of the courses or anything like that, so I had to organise those.

I became Detective Inspector in October 1992 and so by December 1992 I was just really finding my feet at Islington police station in my new role. It was one of those situations where you get thrown in the deep end...

I'd learned from being promoted to inspector at a very young age and young in service that the worst thing you can do when you're thrown into a situation like that is to pretend you know something. You have to be able to ask and soak up things and learn quickly. I was lucky enough to have some colleagues there, the DIs, who were receptive to me. And you know, I think I played it ever so humble. I went there, admitted that I knew very little and I was there to learn from them; they understood that and took it on board.

It would have been easy to be resented. But I was hopefully smart enough to understand that and tried to make sure that I didn't fall into that trap. The Met would have a dozen people a year that would go onto that scheme. And some of them went with a visible sense of arrogance or a sense of entitlement, and I didn't ever want to do that.

My dad was a copper, a PC, and he was of great help in saying to me, you need to work hard and show you're good at what you do. And then people won't mind the fact that you've been given this opportunity and advantage that others don't get. I took that to heart.

I understood very quickly that if you were to succeed, then you needed to make sure that you treated those who were working with you well in a way that encouraged them to work.

And as time went on, when I became Senior Investigating Officer (SIO) in charge of a murder squad, I would say that was the major part of my role. People would think that the major part was setting the strategy of investigating murders – and that was a lot of it. But the main thing, most important of all, was to provide the right conditions so that the people on my team could do the best possible job they could. And that meant understanding them and understanding what they needed and what they needed to work and to be effective.

I think the attitude was about them, about the task, rather than about me. That stood me in good stead.

It's the same as when I was the young inspector at Leyton. I told these experienced sergeants that I was new to this: "I'm going to make mistakes if I go blundering on, so I'm going to lean on you." And I think they appreciated the honesty – we made it work.

When I went to Islington, I was living out at Hoddesdon in Hertfordshire. I was married, I had a daughter who was coming up to four - and she would have been four that Christmas day. And my son was born in

August, 1992. So I had a two-month-old when I went, and a nearly four-year-old. Interestingly enough, one of the things I remember when I was first there, we had a Sudden Infant Death Syndrome case, something that the DIs had to go out to. The DCI came in and asked me to go to it and I sort of got up and John Creese, one of the other DIs there, came over and took a piece of paper out of my hand and said: “You're not going, I'm going to that,”, because he knew that I had a two-month old baby at home. It’s little things like that you remember; you remember people's kindness but also astuteness. You know, for him to realise that actually, “no, Colin's not the person to turn out that because he's got a baby at home”.

It's little bits like that you pick up all the time and you file away, you think: “I’ll remember that in the future.” You need to have this appreciation of what your officers are – they’re not just your colleagues they're not just coppers, they're actually ordinary people with home lives and things going on. And you need to be aware of that so you can help them through.

My first wife was a police officer herself. When I took up the opportunity to go and be a detective, we talked about the fact that it would mean a difference in my working habits. But she appreciated it was something that I really wanted to do. I mean, in some ways, doing shift work is not greatly conducive to family life, but neither was being a uniformed inspector. At least as a detective, rather than having one weekend off in four, I was getting five weekends off in six. There were swings and roundabouts to it. But did it mean I didn't spend as much time with my kids when they were very young? Probably. Now my son's a police officer, he's got two young children, two boys, both under four years old. His wife is a police officer too and they've both made career choices to try and fit in around their family life.

But I think the opportunity to do that in the police is far better in 2024 than it ever was in 1992 – my first wife had to essentially give up policing, because there wasn't any way, if she'd wanted to go back to work after she'd had her first child, she'd have had to have gone back to doing full-time – early mornings, late nights. We looked at the idea of getting a live-in nanny or something like that, even that was so fraught with difficulties because of the night duties and shifts. You can work opposite shifts and that's great in terms of being able to work out your childcare but in terms of being able to see each other and spend time together; you become like ships in the night. We didn't have sort of text messages and things back then. Before I went to Holloway full-time, I was there temporarily and on completely opposite shifts to Maxine, my first wife, and we literally communicated by Post-it notes. You write something on the Post-it and stick it on the fridge door. It's tough and how much effect did that have on how the marriage panned out? I don't know. You know, if I'd have been doing something a bit less demanding then maybe things would have be better but if you're doing something you love and want to then you're a happier person generally anyway.

There wasn't yet a permanent Major Crime Investigation team in the Metropolitan Police like the one I would go on to lead. Murder and serious investigations were overseen by a detective superintendent, and they had an assistant who was a detective sergeant who's known affectionally as the bagman or bagwoman; it goes back to the days when the superintendents were on call to go all over the country as Scotland Yard got called into small forces to help solve crimes – that didn't happen anymore but the term bagman, or bag-lady, still stood.

It was a steep learning curve for me, but there was an acceptance that next time there was a murder on the division that I would be the deputy SIO. I remember being called out to this case vividly, because it was the first murder I had been involved with as a DI. It just so happened that I had injured my neck and was in quite a lot of pain in my chest and in the middle of the night, I'd gone to the local A&E.

I was in the hospital when I got the call out by pager. It went off while I was lying there attached to all these machines. I heard a bleeping noise and, to be honest, I was quite worried. I looked around wondering where the noise was coming from, before realising it was my pager and they wanted me to call in. I phoned the station and they said: "There's been a fire with a body discovered and it's very suspicious." I'd only been a DI for about two months, so it had to be agreed with my boss that I would be the DI on the next murder that happened on the division. It was three days before Christmas and I was looking at something like 12 family members all coming around for Christmas lunch that year. "I'm going to be working," I thought. And that's how it turned out.

A body had been discovered by the fire brigade in a house in a terrace overlooking a playing field in Islington, north London. They were nice expensive houses and this particular one was split into two flats, with the fire and body found in the back room of the upstairs flat.

They'd been called by the neighbours to a fire; when they entered the flat to put the blaze out, they found there was a body. It was obviously suspicious from the very start because there were three knives protruding from his chest.

The first morning was taken up with meeting John Chaplin, the Superintendent who was overseeing it and some forensic people at the flat. The seat of the fire was under the bed where the body's legs were lying. This was hugely suspicious too. It was pretty obvious that whoever had stabbed and killed him had also then tried to set fire to the place to destroy evidence. It's a pretty callous thing to do given that you've got people living downstairs and it was also in a terrace.

Although it was the first murder that I'd been to as a DI investigating a suspicious death, I'd been to similar scenes in the past as a uniformed officer and it was one of those where you had to almost forget that what was in front of you was a human being and that another human being had done that to him. There was a job to be done and we had to get on with it, even though it was obviously a tragic case – you had a man who was by all accounts a gentle, intelligent, cultured man who had been stabbed and set fire to in his own bed.

I was used to seeing dead bodies. I started my first day out of training school, at a police station, as an operational police officer, at 2pm, and by 2.10 I was in the mortuary. You're dealing with sudden deaths and all sorts of things, particularly when you're new and young, so you make sure you just go and do it. Over the following years, I lost count of the number of dead bodies I saw. The difference with this was that for the first time, I had the responsibility of actually trying to work out how it happened and why it happened. Whereas in the past, even as a uniformed inspector going along to a suspicious death, all you're really worried about is making sure you preserve that crime scene. You call the experts and the detectives down, and that's your job.

The fact that it was a pretty horrific situation didn't really faze me or impact me because I'd seen them before and seen worse to be honest. But the realisation that actually it's down to you to piece it all back together and try to work out what happened – that's a new responsibility that was pretty demanding.

The victim, Duncan Bone, was in his early 50s. He was an educated man, and he had a good job as a senior administrator in an NHS trust, working in a hospital in west London. He liked his opera, he liked his music, he liked his drink – too much unfortunately, as he had had some alcohol dependency issues in the past. He lived alone, he had family that he saw and kept in touch with. He was a gay man in a relationship, but he didn't live with his partner. He was well liked and cherished at the place where he worked, and also by his neighbours in Islington.

His partner was clearly distraught at the news. You've always got to look at people close to the victims – so many murders are the result of domestic strife, and you've always got to eliminate that as early as possible. He was obviously absolutely devastated when we spoke to him, and it soon became clear he had a cast iron alibi for that night; he wasn't involved in Duncan's murder.

We knew that Duncan had left work, he'd been at work that evening, got on a tube train to come home and beyond that we didn't know much.

In those days there wasn't the CCTV coverage and mobile phone data and things that investigators rely on so much these days. It was much more a job of trying to see people, talk to people, do the old-fashioned shoe leather detective work.

House-to-house enquiries gave us the first break, because one of the neighbours said that he'd seen two youngish white men going into the flat at about 11 o'clock the previous evening.

Aside from the two white men seen going in, the other break we got was that there was a landline telephone in the flat. We found there was a phone call out to a number he wouldn't normally have called, and the timing fitted in very well with these two white men going in to the flat at about 11pm.

So, there was obviously a line of inquiry there that we could pursue – it turned out they had booked a minicab to flee the scene, although we couldn't trace the driver, so it was a dead end.

It was quite clear in the scene that there had been theft, that things had been taken. We knew we were dealing with a murder which had happened in the course of a robbery, or at least that's what it seemed like to us, with two white men as the suspects.

As the search went through the flat, the team noticed more and more things were missing, the video recorder and cassettes that went with it, records, things like that. It became obvious that there was something else missing from Duncan Bone's personal possessions – his bank card, cheque card, cheque book, any kind of financial instrument that could be used to access his money.

He was a very tidy and meticulous man and he'd kept his bank statements together, so from that we were easily able to find out who he banked with and then to talk to them about any activity on that account.

We found that Duncan Bone's cheques had been used to purchase goods at a time not only after he'd been dead, but actually after we'd turned up at the scene, while we were there completing the search for the scene. Somebody was out using the victim's cheque book and card to buy things.

It was a pretty good assumption that whoever was cashing those cheques and was using Duncan Bone's money knew something about the way he had been killed.

This line of inquiry around Duncan Bone's bank account suddenly became the most attractive and important element. We knew we were looking for two white men but there were a lot of those in London at the time, we needed something more focused and this financial line gave us that.

There was a sports shop in the centre of Northampton where Duncan Bone had apparently bought some trainers the morning after his death. Keith Manktelow, who was a very experienced DS from Islington, went up with a colleague to Northampton. They spoke to the shopkeeper and he said: "Yes, we remember these two men coming in and using these cheques."

This was good, but he was absolutely adamant that it was a white man and a black man together, and not two white men as the neighbours had said. Keith pushed him on this and made sure he was absolutely certain, and he said: "Yeah, I'm absolutely certain, I remember it, here's the receipt, here's the details, you can see where they've used his card, but I can't really tell you any more than that."

A cleaner working the shop windows then confirmed that a traffic warden was putting tickets on cars parked outside on the day in question. A good officer will get a little snippet of information and act on it, go and develop it. It's sensible, it's how investigations sometimes work and it's what they did. They went to the local police station and asked: "Do you run the traffic wardens?"

"Yes," they said.

"Do they work out of here?"

"Yes."

"Who worked on the town centre on this road?"

From this, they were able to speak to the traffic warden for that road. He went through his notebook and said: "Oh yes, 9.10am or something." He had the time, and added: "This day, this is the car, I did put a ticket on it, here's the registration number."

The registration number was checked and came back as registered to a lady living in Waltham Abbey, Essex. It was a Talbot Solara car – there weren't many of those about at the time, let alone now, and it was grey green.

This caused a degree of excitement, we now had something tangible. We had someone to speak to who had been using Duncan Bone's cheques and cards. Officers went down to Waltham Abbey and spoke to this lady, but the excitement soon petered out. She said: "Yes, it was my car, I did have it for a long time, but I put it into the auctions at Chingford a couple of months ago and it got sold through there." This was December 22 or 23 and the car auctions were shut until new year.

There was no way in that short time that we could get access to see who had bought this car.

In the meantime, the best thing we could do was to put what's known as an interest report on that car's registration number. If any police officer in the country does a check on the registration number of that car, there will be a flag that said: "The murder squad at Islington wants to talk about this car because it was involved in a serious crime."

We soon got a telephone call to say: "The car has been stopped by police." A uniformed officer, a traffic officer on a motorcycle on Dalston Lane, east London, had seen the car, thought there might be something suspicious about it, performed a check on the Police National Computer, and hit our flag. He was there, he had the car stopped, he had the driver there, he was a black man. We had someone to talk to.

The driver of the car stopped in Dalston Lane was a man called David Komolafe. "I don't know what you're talking about," he said when it was put to him that he was involved in some murder.

"This is not something we can sort out on the street on Dalston Lane, you're being arrested."

So, he was arrested on suspicion of murder, and we got to talk to him, and it turned out David Komolafe was involved in a minicab firm which had its office in Dalston.

David Komolafe said: "No way was I involved in the murder, I don't know anything about any murder." He said the woman who was a controller at night in the minicab office had a brother called Colin Lockett. He'd been staying with his sister, but they'd fallen out. His behaviour had been such that she didn't want him to live there anymore, and she kicked him out. Lockett was effectively homeless, Komolafe thought he had been living at hostels.

On the morning after Duncan Bone was murdered, Colin Lockett came to Komolafe with a lot of his possessions – Duncan Bone's possessions – and asked him if he would store some of them at his house for him. As payment for this favour, Lockett said he had a cheque book and card, and they could go out together shopping. And that's what they did. David Komolafe took the possessions and stored them at his home and he and Colin Lockett had gone in the Talbot Solara up to Northampton because they thought by going out of London it would throw us off the scent.

We went to see Colin Lockett's sister in the cab office in Dalston. She couldn't really help us, but it was clear there was no love lost between her and her brother. As she said: "Yeah he's been living with me, he was a pain, I kicked him out."

We asked her if he'd left any things at her house and she said: "Yeah, he probably has as he's been living there for a bit, but be my guest, come around and have a look and you can go through the things that he left."

In this search, officers found some paperwork from a hostel in Spitalfields, east London, called Providence Lane. It was clear that he'd had some contact with them and possibly even lived or stayed there in the past. It became our next place of inquiry. We went there and the staff were very helpful: "Oh yeah, we know this man, we know Colin Lockett, he has lived here, but he doesn't live here at the moment, he went away, I think he went to live with his sister." It corroborated that we had the right man. We knew it was Colin Lockett and David Komolafe and they were a white man and a black man. Maybe the eyewitness at the house was wrong. The priority was clearly to find Colin Lockett.

We got a phone call from the staff at the Providence Lane hostel: "You did ask us if Colin Lockett got in touch, would we tell you? He phoned up today asking if we could give him a bed."

This was fantastic. We'd got him.

"Great, is he still there now?"

"Oh, no, we haven't got any space. It's Christmas and we're full up, we've referred him to a number of other agencies that might be able to help him but we couldn't."

There was a frantic spin through multiple copies of Yellow Pages to find all the hostels and Crisis at Christmas and other homeless charities in the area. We phoned all of them up and said: "If this man phones you up, can you please tell us so we can find him."

It was Christmas Eve. The afternoon wore on and it got to six o'clock, seven o'clock, and people started to go home for Christmas. There was little else we could do. There was just a handful of us, three or four of us left in the office at about half past eight on Christmas Eve evening.

The phone rang and it was a worker from one of the charities we'd spoken to. "Oh you wanted to know about Colin Lockett, he's phoned us to see if we had a bed for the night."

"Well, where is he? Where did you place him?"

"Well, we haven't yet. He's hanging on the other line, because we're trying to find somewhere for him. It's Christmas and it's very difficult'.."

"Well, do you know where he is?"

"He's told us he's at Euston Station, he's on a payphone at Euston and we've got the number in case he gets cut off."

Euston Station is not that far from Islington Police Station, where we were. But even at half past eight on Christmas Eve, it's a journey that would normally take 10 minutes or so, we probably didn't have 10 minutes.

We asked the charity worker to not lose Lockett. "Can you keep Colin Lockett on the phone, tell him anything, tell him your computer's gone down, tell him you're having trouble getting through, it's engaged or something like that, but just keep him on that phone."

Officers jumped into a police car, and they made it in about three minutes. They went into the concourse at Euston Station and there, on one of the payphones, was Colin Lockett.

They knew it was him, because we had an e-fit sketch done of the two men the witness had seen at the house. They had that with them, and for once, the likeness was pretty good. Officers told me as soon as they saw this man on the phone and looked at the e-fit, they knew they had the right man. It was nine o'clock Christmas Eve and we had our first suspect in custody.

Colin Lockett was interviewed and he again, perhaps understandably, wanted to distance himself from the murder and the arson. He told us the story that he had been begging at King's Cross in the railway station. Duncan Bone had approached him, talked to him, and invited him back to his flat back in Islington and Lockett had accompanied him willingly.

He was honest about his plans: "I intended from the very start, to rob this man who was taking me back to his house, that's what I wanted to do."

Lockett continued: "When I got back there, it became clear that he wanted sex, and that wasn't something I was going to do, but I did know somebody who I thought might and might come and help, and that was a friend of mine, I phoned him."

Lockett told us he'd said to his friend: "'I'm with this man in the flat, we can get in there easy because he's happy and he thinks he's going to have sex with you, and we can rob him."

When the man turned up, Lockett went out and met him and took him in.

"Was that David Komolafe?" we asked immediately.

"No, it wasn't him, it was a white man, it was somebody called Karl Warne."

All of a sudden, we realised our eyewitness was correct – at 11 o'clock on the night of the murder and arson, there were two young white men going into Duncan Bone's flat.

The intention of Colin Lockett was still very much to rob him, but Duncan Bone thought that he was going to have sex with Karl. "I sat in the living room and was disconnecting a video and things that we stole, and Karl was in the bedroom with him and the next thing I know, I hear this kerfuffle and go in and find that Karl Warne had stabbed Duncan Bone on his bed and had killed him, I had nothing to do with it, I was in the other room at the time."

According to him, Lockett told us he knew nothing about it. He just heard a noise, went, and found his friend had stabbed this man five times, leaving knives protruding from his chest.

They took what they could, including his bank cards. They used his holdall and suitcase to put their loot in, including the video recorder. And then they set a fire, a small fire under the bed to attempt to cover their tracks.

We asked him more about what happened after he and Warne left the flat. he said that they'd gone to King's Cross where they sold the video recorder to a man in a pub. They then made their way to Camden Town where they got a minicab to take them to Providence Lane hostel, Spitalfields. Was it his sister's firm? "No, no it was another firm at Camden Town tube station and all I can remember is that it was a brown car."

We now had two lines of inquiry that would enable us to corroborate Colin Lockett's story. Firstly we had to find the brown minicab from Camden Town that ferried them to Spitalfields; secondly, we had to try and find the man who bought the video recorder from them in Kings Cross in the pub. I went with a couple of officers to Camden Town and Keith Manktelow went with some other officers to the pub in Kings Cross.

We went up to Camden Town at lunchtime on Christmas Day, and, as luck would have it, there sitting outside the cab office is a brown Austin Maestro. We went and spoke to the driver, and he said it rang a bell, but to check in the office, as they kept details of all journeys. And yes, they were able to produce the records which showed that the man outside in the brown Maestro had taken two white men and a load of property with them over to Spitalfields to the Providence Lane hostel.

Keith Manktelow went to the pub where eventually the landlord of the pub said he knew and named the man who bought the video recorder. He remembered the incident and the man was duly summoned and came along to the pub with the video recorder, which we recovered. As far as we could work out and were able to check, everything Colin Lockett had told us was true.

The next thing we had to do was to arrest Karl Warne.

It proved to be relatively easy. We went over to Providence Lane, the hostel, and there he was. Warne was arrested and his space and locker in the hostel were searched. In the locker was an envelope, with Karl Warne's name on it. And when we looked inside it what did we find? Duncan Bone's cheque card and cheque book. In addition to this envelope containing Duncan Bone's cheques and cards, we found a holdall and a suitcase that were Duncan Bone's and, best of all, the cab driver that had taken Lockett and Warne from Camden to Providence Lane, was able to identify those as the ones the two men he'd driven had brought into the car with them.

The case was starting to come together.

After his arrest, Karl Warne was taken to Islington Police Station where he was interviewed, and he chose to make no comment to everything that was spoken to him. Despite him not telling us, the evidence from Lockett, the corroboration and the things we found at Lockett's former place meant there was ample evidence. Both men were charged on Boxing Day and appeared in court the day after.

The investigation had all taken place within the space of four days over Christmas, We knew pretty much everything that happened that night.

Warne, on advice of the CPS, was charged with murdering Duncan Bone and both men were charged with conspiracy to rob and another offence of arson. The case was almost closed then, there was little more that we could do. We had found every piece of evidence that was available, all within the space of a few days. What we didn't know of course was how they were going to handle the trial and what their defences were likely to be. Was Karl Warne was going to try to say it was all Colin Lockett's fault? It's what's known as a cutthroat defence where you have two defendants and each accuses the other.

Clearly, Colin Lockett was accusing Karl Warne as the murderer and everything we found suggested that was true, but we didn't know what Karl Warne was going to say. Komolafe had also been charged with dishonesty and deception, using Bone's cards and pleaded guilty – he was given 12 months' probation.

Lockett was eventually jailed for seven years with the judge remarking: "You were present in the flat while Mr Bone was being brutally and callously stabbed to death and you departed with the spoils."

But the main event was Karl Warne's trial for murder. Lockett gave his evidence in that trial as we thought he would, but Warne didn't accuse Lockett of the murder. Instead, he admitted that he had stabbed Duncan Bone. You might think that somebody who stabbed another person five times, leaving three knives stuck in that man's chest as he dies, has got a difficult job saying that wasn't a murder.

But Karl Warne was a man who through his childhood had been through the care system and had been, as he said, abused on numerous occasions. This had given him a pathological fear and hatred of gay men and gay sex. He said when he saw Duncan Bone undressed, preparing for sex, something flipped in his head.

All those bad memories came back and he was just driven to kill him. He said: "I'm guilty of manslaughter by reason of diminished responsibility." Essentially, he was saying that he was so affected by what was going on, by something that happened to him, that he temporarily lost control of his mind, of what he was doing. And, although he killed someone, he shouldn't be convicted of murdering them, instead it's manslaughter.

The reason Karl Warne and many other people make this admission is because with a manslaughter conviction and a plea of guilty, the judge has flexibility; he has discretion in the sentence, whereas if there is a conviction for murder, there has to be a life sentence. You can be sentenced to life for manslaughter but that's often not the case.

The jury failed to agree on the murder charge but found Warne guilty of manslaughter on grounds of provocation. Jailing the pair, Judge Kenneth Richardson QC said, 'This was a wanton, vicious and cold blooded killing, far from being immobilised with horror at what had happened, you stole a large quantity of Mr Bone's property, only a custodial sentence is adequate to protect the public from serious harm'.

He sentenced Warne to 14 years in prison, telling him: "You are a psychopath and likely to be for the foreseeable future."

We'd had a series of attacks on gay men, murders, committed by the serial killer Colin Ireland. And I suppose then you can trace through to a few years later almost to things like Copeland and the Admiral Duncan bombing, so this period was a pretty tough one for crimes against gay men.

It was one of those cases where you realise after you know who the people are and who you've charged and what they were doing, that actually they would have carried on. It was something that increased and I became more acutely aware of as my career as a detective progressed. Justice and retribution or revenge or punishment is all very well. I think a lot of people and a lot of police officers think about that, I did at the time, as the primary goal of what we do.

But actually when you're talking about murders and serious assaults, and particularly when they're on strangers, there's a huge dimension to it, which is the protection of the rest of the public.

And it was only really after Levi Bellfield was convicted that I realised that was probably the most important thing in what we did – to take these people out of the game so that they couldn't create any more victims. There are some murders and assaults that happen because of the two people involved – the killer and the victim. And if they weren't those two people, the person is no risk to anybody else, particularly where there's a relationship between the two people. But in the ones where the victims are essentially random or victims of some other sort of crime like they were in the Duncan Bone case then there's this knowledge that people don't just do it once and stop, they carry on.

CHAPTER 2
THE DREAM CITY CINEMA FIRE

When you're on a murder squad and there weren't any murders happening, you'd be seconded to other things or you'd help out on this or that. There was always an element of sitting around twiddling your thumbs waiting for something to happen.

After the Duncan Bone murder, I wrote what they used to call the report – essentially the document that goes to the Crown Prosecution Service, a brief for counsel – and I got a lovely letter back from the CPS saying how well I'd done it. At least then I knew I could actually write and put the arguments together and marshal them. We were also working on changing policing to the "sector model". I'd worked on that at Holloway as an inspector and they wanted it done at Islington so I did that as well.

And I then got seconded from the normal office to Operation Welwyn. It was a multi-agency thing between the Met, British Transport Police and the London boroughs of Camden and Islington, aimed at ridding

King's Cross of the scourge of drug dealing and sex workers and dirty bookshops.

There was a uniform team that worked on the street with sex workers and the porno book shops and things. And then there was a detective team which worked on drug dealers.

I was not all that keen to do it. I've never really taken a great deal of interest in drug-dealing as a sort of a crime type, although obviously I dealt with it when I came across it, but it was my turn to go. And in the event I learned so, so much from the 18 months on Operation Welwyn.

I was still working out of Islington, but it was good, there was a lot of proactive work done, a lot of plain clothes work – scruffy plain clothes work. I was charged for the first time with handling test purchase officers. We had cameras put in around Kings Cross station, looking at the post office across the road from the station, and the various shops. You could look over at the post office and there'd be six drug dealers standing outside – they were all mostly crack, but a lot of heroin as well. They kept it in their mouth and passed it on by kissing, although sometimes they kept them in other orifices.

We sent these young – and they were really young – officers in to buy heroin and crack. It's no good sending 45-year-old blokes with a bald head and a paunch down to buy drugs, it doesn't work. So new and relatively inexperienced officers who had been trained to do it would go along and buy drugs. We were filming, and we'd do that for about six weeks, then we'd put it all together. We didn't know who these people were, we gave them all nicknames. We had Buckle Shoes and Rainbow Jacket and stuff like that. We'd then get the uniform team to help us and we'd send the officers in scruffy plain clothes out on the streets. We'd all be in this control room at the station looking at our cameras and monitors and then we'd see Buckle Shoes over there and he needed arresting. We'd get the camera on them and then you'd send the uniform team in, who'd do it just like it's an ordinary stop in the street. Buckle Shoes himself would be thinking: "Well, they've not seen me do anything. I've not sold any drugs for half an hour. I've got it all in my mouth or secreted somewhere else. I'm pretty fireproof and there could be no conflicts at all." And they just say: "You're being nicked for supplying heroin."

"When? What?"

And we'd tell them over the radio: "It was on November 23, maybe six, eight weeks before. We'd got a file of facts of what they were doing at any given time. And so we'd whizz them all in and they would all go to prison.

We had one officer who managed to buy Kendall mint cake instead of crack cocaine not once but three times. We found a way around it because there's actually an offence of making an offer to supply. And it's exactly the same punishment as supplying, the courts treat it exactly as if they had sold controlled drugs.

There was one dealer – in fact it was Buckle Shoes himself – where we actually watched him go in the shop, buy a four-finger KitKat, unwrap it, eat it all, throw the paper wrapper on the floor, then screw the foil wrapper up into a tight ball and sell it to a police officer for a tenner. He went to prison for four years – for selling a KitKat wrapper and "making an offer to supply".

I really, really enjoyed it and I learned tons. I learned so much about undercover work; that's what I did in between those two murders, the one of Duncan Bone and the Dream City Cinema.

I don't think the fire at the Dream City Cinema is given as much attention and sits in the history of London as an event of the magnitude that it was. Eleven people died in one night in one place.

And very few people are aware that a mass murder took place in St John Street on the edge of the city of London 1994 – more people died there than in almost any other single act excluding terrorism in the last century.

Even for the officers dealing with it, it was far beyond what even hardened police detectives were used to – the sheer scale of death in one incident like this.

It was late in February, I was divisional DI at Islington, although not on call – I was at home on a Saturday evening. I got a call from Eddie O'Connell, who was my DCI at the time who said: "Can you come in, we've had a bit of a fire."

That was one of the biggest understatements I think I've ever come across in my police career.

"I'm not on call, somebody else is on call," I replied.

"No, we need you all in, it's big, it's something that's going to need all of us."

I drove into Islington and the first thing that I remember was going into my office. I was one of four DIs at the time, still working on Operation Welwyn at Kings Cross. We were based in the incident room and my desk was there. And there, sitting at my desk, was Tony

Comben who was the Commander of the area. I knew it had to be something big if someone of his rank was out in uniform on a Saturday night.

"Hello sir, what brings you out at this time of night? It must be serious," I said.

"I'm just worried somebody famous like a politician might be involved in this," he replied,

At that stage, I didn't know what the job was, but I then quickly found out. There was a cinema on the edge of Smithfield, based in the upper three stories of a terraced block with a shop beneath it. It was a cinema which specialised in pornographic films and it had caught fire. It was unlicensed, it had no proper fire certificate and no means of exit for the scores of men trapped in the inferno.

It turns out the cinema wasn't licensed by the local authority because it had failed the conditions to be licensed and in some ways that meant there was no control over it at all. The trouble is, when a premises is completely unlicensed, then there is no incentive for those who run it to operate within any rules or to adhere to any laws. They simply don't have a licence, it's a rogue establishment. And that's why the fire exits were not sufficient; why it was so difficult for the people inside to get out and away from the fire and to a degree, for the fire brigade to get in and fight the blaze.

The fire had happened on a night when they catered for gay men. It wasn't like that all the time but that particular performance and showings on that day were for that demographic. This created an additional problem – we had to be discreet in how we dealt with the enquiries, not least with the families of those injured or dead, because they might not have known what they were doing there or why they were there. Things were sadly less enlightened back then, far fewer gay people were comfortable with being “out”.

There was certainly a feeling within the police at the time that the incident had to be handled with a great deal of sensitivity in terms of not only dealing with the victims' families, but the way in which it was presented in the media, because this was 1994 and in 1994 things were very different in some ways to what we see now in the 2020s.

There were chilling tales coming from people involved and the most horrific stories of people trying to escape the blaze, throwing themselves out of windows to flee, others burning or being knocked out by smoke inhalation in situ, fire escapes being chained up or non-existent. Perhaps even more horrific was the fact those trapped in the inferno were faced with the choice of staying in a burning smoke-filled room or jumping out the second-floor window. You just imagine the terror and fear that's going through people's minds as you try to make that decision quickly, under pressure. You were damned if you do and damned if you don't.

There was a furniture delivery van nearby and its driver saw what was happening and manoeuvred it, quite bravely, to the burning building so people could come out through the upper windows onto the top of the van to escape. There was one man who couldn't bring himself to leap out of the window so he found a crack in the floorboards. He was lying on the floor with his nose in this crack in the floorboards trying to get clean air from the room below to breathe. It must have been an absolutely horrific experience to be in this place, trapped, there were flames coming up the stairs, there was no way out, what could you do?

The fire service were there quite quickly and they had a turntable ladder and the fire fighters were telling stories of people inside literally fighting, climbing over each other to get down the ladder because there were so many people in there. Such was the panic and the danger.

It was known at that point that there were fatalities, more than one, but also there was a number of injured who had been taken to hospital who, it was really thought, might not make it. The worry was that it wasn't going to be one or two deaths, more that it was going to be half a dozen, maybe even more.

It was all hands to the pumps, every spare officer that could be dragged in from home from the detective force at Islington Division was called in to deal with it. One of our first tasks was to find exactly where they were being treated because there were so many from this one incident, they had been taken to hospitals all across the London area. It was a really difficult time that night, driving around essentially most of the casualty departments in north and east London and even out to Billericay to the burns unit. I heard stories that will stay with me forever, meeting people who were telling us how terrified they'd been, how they had feared for their lives and jumped from windows, struggled through a burning building, the panic that was there amongst all the people who were in the cinema at the time. One man said it was every man for himself in there, he said people were walking over other people to try to get out because they knew if they didn't get out of that building, they were going to die. It was far beyond what even hardened detectives and hardened police officers were used to, this scale of death in one incident like this.

We were trying to do a headcount of victims and of people who were injured and who had died. A lot of the victims were still alive that Saturday evening, a lot of the people who died took some hours to die and were conscious. We were talking to them and when we finally finished it was in the hours of the morning. I had a few hours of sleep and then returned to duty, to the news that people we had been sitting at the bedside talking to just a few hours before had died. That's something that you don't often encounter as a murder detective, because normally by the time you arrive, the deed has been done and someone has already died.

I was kind of aware that's how burn injuries work, but it didn't occur to me when I was talking to these people and asking what happened, with them saying "I was just watching the film and all of a sudden there's loads of shouting loads of smoke", that the next day they would be dead. That, less than 24 hours after I was chatting with them, they are being dissected in front of you. Certainly, one of my colleagues at the time, it had a real effect on him, he found it really difficult to cope with work afterwards and he didn't stay much longer in the police service.

It turned out that 11 men lost their life that night, 15 had been injured and hospitalised, but only four of those survived.

Across the 11 victims and the other men who were injured – all the victims of this crime – there was a real cross-section of society. Their age ranged from their 20s to their 60s, we had engineers, we had white-collar workers, we had single people, we had out gay people, we had people who were married and weren't out, it was a real cross-section. The fact that they were in an unlicensed sex cinema and watching pornographic films just wasn't an issue, we were dealing with something much more serious than that.

My investigation strand was to do with the victims, so I ended up at St Pancras Mortuary on the Sunday morning. We had two pathologists, two slabs, two photographers, two scenes of crime officers and we did all 11 post-mortem examinations in one day. Not all of the men had identification on them, it took us a while. One of them I think we didn't identify for a couple of weeks. Mostly, we found out who they were, eventually, even if this was 1994 and gay men couldn't be as open about their life and their sexuality in those days, that's just how things sadly were.

There was no question of DNA, so post-mortems could be carried out quite quickly. It wouldn't be possible these days to do 11 in one go, even with two slabs running parallel. It was a real experience in many ways – you get used to dealing with death eventually, but this was at the beginning of my career as a murder squad detective and to have so much of it in one place at one time was heartbreaking. These were just men who had been out on a Saturday evening for entertainment, and they ended up having to throw themselves out of a building and died or died of smoke inhalation. It was a pretty sombre atmosphere.

There was a real logistical difficulty of doing so many post-mortems in the same building on the same day.

We had two pathologists, two scenes of crime officers, two photographers, two exhibits officers. It was so difficult to manage that you almost forgot what you were dealing with, who the people were. The most bizarre thing I remember is that we did six and we all stopped and went to McDonald's – the fact that you could actually go and eat something, and then come back and do that. It was a very different and difficult sort of situation.

I knew it was going to be unpleasant, so before I left that morning I deliberately put on an old pair of jeans and an old jumper. After we'd done these post-mortems, the clothes had the stench of death, the smell of the fire on them. I knew that no matter how many times I washed them, they'd still have that smell, I'd know it was there, I'd think it was there even if it really wasn't. They would always be a reminder of that particularly harrowing day. It was the only time I ever did this, but as soon as I got home, I took the clothes off and they went straight in the bin. There was no point in washing them. No matter how clean, to me, they would have been, they would have always reminded me of that night.

It was one of those days where you went home and you just hoped your family didn't ask: "What did you do at work today Dad?" How can you explain that you were standing there while eleven people who had just been killed are being examined? We tried to deal with the victims as sensitively and as sympathetically as we could and that included a conscious decision on our part that we were not going to out them as having been at an unlicensed cinema watching gay porn. We thought it might have an effect on public sympathy at the time – we had been asking for witnesses and we didn't want to do anything that would make the public less willing to help us in trying to find out what had happened. It caused us difficulties because we didn't know who some of the victims were, they didn't have ID documents with them. We would normally use publicity, we would normally go public with the media, newspapers and the local news with a message: "We don't know who this person is, and we think he is a victim." We needed to be careful around that because what you don't want to do is double the suffering.

We really needed to be careful in trying to establish the identities of the men. We wanted to avoid what could have been effectively telling family and friends not only "oh, he's dead", but also "by the way, this is what he was doing when he died". You don't want to load almost two levels of suffering to family and friends.

There was another worry at the time – a fear that someone from, say, the judiciary or the government might have been there that night, adding further embarrassment. Fortunately, that wasn't the case, so we didn't have that added dimension to the investigation, but we still had nearly two dozen victims who were either dead or critically injured that needed dealing with, needed identifying and their families had to be informed.

The fact that the victims of this crime represented such a real cross-section of society fed into this belief we had that we needed to be very careful about what we said about these people and we had to be careful that they couldn't be identified.

It would have been gratuitous to just give their names to the media for the sake of it, we didn't need to for the investigation. We kept their anonymity.

The next thing to do, after the post-mortems and victim interviews, was to investigate the fire. How did the fire start? Where did the fire start? This would be the starting point for our investigations. We also had initial reports from people working at the cinema, as well as attendees.

These suggested that there had been a disagreement on the ground floor, by the entrance/ticket office. One of their regular customers, known only as Deaf Dave – he was deaf-mute and obviously the cinema had no records of its members – had turned up. He was probably a bit drunk on the night and had tried to gain admission but had been refused on the grounds that it was gay films showing and they knew it wasn't what he was into. We think there may have been a communication issue between Dave being deaf and not understanding.

There was a big argument, he thought they weren't honouring his membership. There was a bouncer of sorts there and he had a bit of an altercation with the bouncer – there was some jostling and a headbutt, and it might even be that the bouncer has assaulted him.

Deaf Dave left, but went to a nearby petrol station, bought a gallon of petrol, and returned to the cinema.

There was a door on the ground floor, you'd go in through that and there was a box office on the right, and then there was a set of stairs that go to the upper floors where the cinema was. He went back there, sloshed the contents of the petrol up the stairs and threw a match into it and set fire to it. What he had also done, probably accidentally, was drop the can as he fled. That can wedged the front door open which created a draft in, a means for the air to rush in up the staircase as it burnt and by all accounts the building just caught fire very, very quickly. Within minutes of him setting it on fire, the whole four-storey building was ablaze.

CCTV at the local Texaco petrol station showed a man coming in and buying a can and a gallon of petrol at just about the right time – 20 minutes after the argument between the bouncer and person who was at the ticket office – had happened.

So, clearly that was our man. And although the club itself didn't have particularly good records of membership, again because it didn't have to because it wasn't licensed, it didn't take very long for inquiries to establish that this was David Lauwers.

Lauwers was an interesting character, he was a tailor's cutter, obviously he had this disability of his hearing and speech, he had originally come from Scotland and settled in north London. He had a few previous convictions, they weren't for anything major, interestingly one of them was for causing criminal damage and when it was looked into, he caused that criminal damage by fire.

Lauwers gave himself up at Walthamstow Police Station. He walked in and said: "I think you're looking for me, I've done something silly."

In some ways I think he was quite remorseful, I think he did what he did on the spur of the moment and he certainly didn't think it through and what the effects might be. He was quite shocked and surprised that his action had caused the death of 11 other men. I don't think he understood and knew that it was gay porn day. I don't think it was a homophobic attack as such, I don't think he understood, I think it was a communication issue – he was just really angry. If it had been communicated to him properly the first time he may have gone away and came back later.

It's kind of unusual in some ways to see this level of remorse, he volunteered himself to police as soon as he realised what he had done and he was in the media, he gave himself up and came into the police station. He'd already said previously to one of his friends: "I could be on a murder charge, I did that, but I was just annoyed." The fact that he showed this remorse was evident in the leniency of the sentence that he got. He pleaded guilty to manslaughter and he was sentenced to life with a recommendation that he must serve at least 10 years before he would be able to apply for parole.

David Lauwers is a little bit unusual in that most homicide cases, murder and manslaughter cases are fought, people don't plead guilty, there's just not much in it for them. I think it was quite appropriate in some ways that he was convicted of manslaughter rather than murder, he didn't intend to kill anybody, he certainly didn't intend to kill 11 people but regardless, what he did was such a reckless act there's no doubt that he was criminally responsible for the deaths.

It's so much more of a tragedy in some ways – it was a stupid overreaction and misunderstanding that caused him to deal with it in such an extreme way. Even then, 11 people in one act is fortunately something you don't see very often. If he had intended to kill these people and the judge thought that they had been murders, his sentence would have been much, much longer.

We always assumed that David Lauwers had essentially lost his temper, was so annoyed that he wasn't allowed in the cinema that he reacted by going and buying some petrol and setting fire to it, just out of temper. Now, sadly we will never be able to ask him, he admitted that he did it, but the reason why he did it, we don't know. He died in prison, so he took the answer to that question to the grave with him.

Given the change in attitudes and change in legal attitudes over the last thirty years, this crime would be viewed very differently today. In 1994, hate crime overall as a concept was in its infancy and certainly in relation to the LGBTQ community really wasn't on the radar of the legal system. Now of course, it's very different and I think these days it would be such a massively aggravating factor that even a defendant who gave himself up and pleaded guilty – which are both things for which you get credit when being sentenced – would find himself looking at a much different outcome than that which followed in this case.

I think if we had a crime like this repeated now, it would be viewed in a very different light and possibly treated much more seriously. There was certainly a feeling within the police at the time that we had to deal with this with a degree of sensitivity, that wasn't because of the victims' families but also the way it was presented in the media because of the prevailing attitudes of the time.

Of course, what we really did at the start was to set the train in motion. By the time you come to the trial, there was an order made that the victims were to remain anonymous. And that anonymity was continued when we got to the trial, these victims have never been identified to this day, the only people who know who the victims were of the fire at Smithfield were their immediate family and the police officers that dealt with it, it didn't go into the public domain.

I'm quite proud of that really, how we managed to achieve that and how we managed to keep at least a little bit of dignity for the victims.

I think looking back at it now a long time afterwards, I think we were ahead of the game in some ways. I think we dealt with these victims in a way and with sensitivity that some might have found unusual at that time. It wasn't typical of the establishment, the authorities or the police then, but we kind of saw that there was this issue, and we took great pains to make sure we didn't cause additional offence or upset for people.

But I really do think that that's meant that this event doesn't have the notoriety in London's history that it deserves. It was just the scale of it, that's what makes it so amazing that so few people know about the case. Within six months, it had gone; nobody remembers it. You talk to people now and say: "I was on a murder investigation with 11 victims." – people wouldn't believe it, they'd say: "Where did that happen? Was it terrorism?"

One of the reasons that it did go under the radar, of course, was that it was a deliberate policy and tactic with the media to be as low key as we could with it because of the risk that people who were there or who even people who had died may have been embarrassed. They would expose them and in some ways that's quite sensitive. it sort of sums up the time.

Back in 1986, I was only 25 years old and an inspector. I got called into the office by my superintendent. He told me he was on his way into work that morning and he saw the area car – a fast response car, a big old Rover. I was thinking what had he seen them doing? He said: "It had two women in it. What are two women doing working on the area car?"

"Well, one's driving, one's working the radio," I replied.

And he grinned and he said: "But they're two women. You could have a male officer getting a kicking, he calls up for assistance and he gets two women!"

To me it just wasn't the way I thought, they were both competent officers, both have the skills to do those two tasks. And it never occurred to me that anyone would think you shouldn't have two women together in a police car. But he was older than my parents, almost two generations removed from me, had been in the forces during the war. He had a different outlook on life. I was the youngest person at my rank in the whole country. I'd grown up with a different understanding.

I was just flabbergasted but it showed me that actually I come from a different generation to those people there and things are going to change.

I stress the point in some ways, there were probably at that time some right, gnarled-up old detectives who had typical working class male attitudes about homosexuality from the 60s and 70s. But none of them wanted to do anything but solve it. None of them wanted to do anything but care for the victims and their families. I think people don't believe it. They don't understand the ability of people doing a job like policing where conflict is a regular part of the world, that they are able to have all the kind of attitudes and thoughts and biases and prejudices of the general population. And yet they put them to one side when they're doing their job because they're professional enough to do just that. And that's why when people of my sort of age and my era are asked: "You must have seen loads of racism, homophobia, sexism and stuff?" Not really, I've seen a bit of sexism internally maybe, towards female officers, but I've never been present on the street where I think somebody's been treated worse because of their sex or their race or their orientation or whatever.

We were trying to change that misconception among people, particularly those who are being police critical, that the quality or status of the victim in murder cases dictates how good the response to the investigation is. Every single murder investigation that I've ever been involved with, every single officer, a man and woman, as a matter of professional pride if not anything else, wants to solve it and do what they can.

If you stopped to think about whether someone's lifestyle or their choices or their sexual orientation or their race or their ethnicity had contributed to their murder or not, then you just get yourself in all sorts of knots and a tangled wrap and you're not doing the job. The old adage I always use is "tell me how he lived, I'll tell you how he died". You have to look at what somebody's life was like to try to get an understanding of the circumstances surrounding the death that might be relevant. But the fact was, if we didn't care about investigating murders of sex workers, or gay people, or drug dealers, or drug users, or homeless people; if we made a value judgment about the way they lived their life and launched our investigation accordingly with as much zeal as we thought that they might, in inverted commas, “deserve”, then we'd be in a really strange place.

I can honestly say that never ever happens. People will say: “Oh you don't care about him because he's black, you don't care about her because she's a sex worker.” It’s just not true. Every single officer wants to solve that case as soon as it lands on their desk.

CHAPTER 3
THE CULLENS ROBBERY

In 1994, I was a DI, based at Islington Police Station.

It was in the early hours of the Tuesday morning after the Easter Monday, I was at home, asleep in bed. When you go on courses they always tell you that when you get a call in the middle of the night to say you'll ring back and make yourself a cup of tea or coffee, whatever your poison is, and wake up before ringing the caller back to see what the situation is. I've never had a problem; I'm up and instantly awake.

I was in bed with my wife – we still had landlines and one phone in the bedroom and one downstairs. If I got called in the middle of the night I'd always go downstairs because I'd be talking and keeping her awake. I ran downstairs, picked the phone up the night duty DC at Islington was a man called Tony Brown, who had quite a distinctive voice, he came from the Midlands, I think. The phone rang and he uttered the immortal words: "We've got a bit of a strange one, guv'nor."

That's the kind of understatement that police officers use when something is not within the usual run of the mill. Most often I could understand the facts pretty quickly but this was something that was going to tax my brain.

He outlined a rather difficult to understand set of circumstances and the upshot seemed to be that there were two men in custody at Islington Police Station, who had been arrested for committing an armed robbery and two attempted murders. He also said that we had two men who had been shot, at close range in the back of the neck, inside a stolen car. The officers thought it was a falling out between an armed robbery gang, but nobody was really sure of the circumstances. Then there was something about the alarm going off at Marks & Spencer nearby.

It all just seemed really confusing. I'd got used to waking up and kind of instantly snapping into consciousness and work mode when I got an early morning call, but this was one of those where I didn't understand what was being said to me. I couldn't work out what had actually happened.

"You know what I'm going to do?" I said to Tony. "I'll give you a call back in five minutes, I'm going to make myself a cup of coffee, make sure I'm properly awake and I'll ring you back with a pen and paper and I'll see if I can understand what's going on."

Five minutes later when I phoned him back, he gave me the exact same story and although I was absolutely awake and full of caffeine, I still couldn't make head nor tail of what had gone on. Nor could he, and that was what was so strange about the circumstances.

It didn't sit right that a gang of robbers, immediately after they'd carried out an armed robbery at a convenience shop - a Cullens, part of a chain across London - had fallen out and two had ended up getting shot. They'd relieved the store, at gunpoint, of about £8,500, the cash takings over the Easter weekend, and it looked as if the gang had fallen out and then two of them had ended up getting shot.

Then there was the Marks & Spencer aspect to contend with. About 40 yards, or maybe even less, from the shop that had been robbed, there was an M&S store. Its burglar alarm had gone off because there was actually somebody else burgling that shop at that same time. It was a police van with officers responding to that alarm that caught the robbers, standing in the road in Chapel Market looking into the bag they'd stolen from Cullens. They'd run off in different directions and the officers had managed to catch two of them; these were the two who had been arrested.

This was a real mess. There's an old saying: "Detectives don't like coincidences." The idea that all of this was a coincidence and there just happened to be two teams, one doing a burglary and one bigger team doing an armed robbery, within 40 yards of each other at the same time, was something we didn't like. We thought there must be a connection.

"Look," I said, "I'll come in. It's now 2am or whatever, we won't call many of the other officers in yet, we will keep them fresh for the morning. But we can work out a plan between us and see if we can get some sort of idea as to what might have gone on."

What we did know was that two men had been shot in a Rover Metro car, that had been stolen earlier in that day from Leyton in east London. One of the men that was shot came from that area, and the other one was a local Islington lad. Their names were Colin Meek and Gary Mullins.

They were kind of low-grade local criminals, getting involved in something like an armed robbery with firearms was a little bit out of their league; it was a bit of a step up from what they were used to doing. Somebody joked that that was pretty obvious given the fact that they used a Metro as their getaway car. It wasn't really the powerful vehicle of choice for coming away from an armed blagging.

Our feeling after a few hours was that the two men in hospital had been accompanied by two or three men. They had gone into the Cullens store armed with a firearm and a CS gas spray and committed the robbery, just before the store closed and with three days-worth of takings in the till, which they had cleaned out. They then ran back into the side street where the Metro was parked, got into the car at which point somebody – we assumed from the gang – had smashed the windows at the rear sides of the Metro and shot them both in the neck while they sat in the front seats.

We didn't know whether or not they were likely to live, they were both still alive, but they had both been shot at close range in the back of the neck, these were potentially life-threatening injuries. We were treating it from the start as if they were likely to die, and to be honest, even if they didn't, clearly shooting somebody in the back of the neck is attempted murder even if they survive.

Colin Meek and Gary Mullins had been taken to St Bartholomew's hospital. We sent officers down there because they were notionally under arrest, having committed a robbery. Both had undergone emergency surgery to remove the .44 slugs in their neck where they'd been shot. Gary Mullins had suffered damage to his spinal cord. Colin Meek on the other hand had also been shot in the spine but had suffered no apparent ill effects other than the actual wound.

We were keen to get whatever evidence we could from the two men but I got a phone call from one of the officers at the hospital who said: "We've got a bit of a problem with the staff down here, could you pop down?" The hospital staff were refusing to hand the bullets over to my officers, on the basis that they said they were still alive and it was their property.

"They came in with it, so they are going to have to allow us to give it to you," the staff said. I kind of understood the logic of it, but it was a situation I'd never encountered before. While we were negotiating with the administrative staff at the hospital, the A&E consultant almost sidled up to me with two plastic bags, each containing a lump of misshapen, bloodied lead. He said: "There you go officer, this is quite ridiculous, take them."

And that's how we got the bullets to put into evidence.

We started to talk to Colin Meek. Almost remarkably, we literally had a bullet in a plastic bag that had pieces of his spinal cord attached to it. But there he was, up and about, talking and seemingly uninjured save for the bullet hole in his neck. It was good for us because it meant we had somebody who could tell us what had actually gone on.

"I'm not going to speak to you until I've spoken to my lawyer," he said. We managed to get him to speak to a lawyer, the upshot was that he wasn't going to tell us what had gone on unless there was a written undertaking from police to say he would not be prosecuted for the robbery.

By this time, Detective Superintendent Harvey had arrived, we'd agreed that in the circumstances our interests were best served in trying to find out what had gone on, who the missing men were. I consulted with a Crown Prosecution Service lawyer. He said: "Yeah, that's absolutely fine." We agreed a wording for a letter, I typed it up and signed it on headed notepaper. It was, effectively, a get out of jail free card for Colin Meek.

I gave it to him and he ran it past his solicitor, and they said it was all good. "Yeah, that sounds watertight, you can go ahead and talk to them now."

"At last!" we thought.

And then Colin Meek said: "I've absolutely no idea what happened, Gary and I went in to do the robbery, we got back into the getaway car and the lights went out."

"Hang on a minute, what about the other people in your team, the people who shot you, who are they, where can we find them?"

"We've no idea, there was just the two of us on the robbery, we were doing it together, but we don't know about anybody else anywhere."

We then had to look at the possibility the people who had shot Meeks and Mullins, who had got away with the spoils of the robbery, had nothing to do with them. If that was the case, what were they doing there with the firearms they used? We had to start admitting the possibility we had two gangs of robbers at the same place at the same time.

Getting the CPS to agree to not prosecuting so we could get some information had really come to nothing. And now there was this mysterious gang in the middle, two of whom were in the cells and we needed really to work on them to find out who they were.

Meanwhile, we were told that there really had been burglars in Marks & Spencer, it wasn't a faulty alarm. So what we had was a ridiculous and quite bizarre situation, but all the facts were telling us was we had one team of two men, Meeks and Mullins, who were doing an armed robbery at Cullens; we had another team probably of two men, who were doing a burglary at Marks & Spencer; and another team of probably four armed men who for some reason were there and had robbed the robbers of what they'd just stolen – all within 30 yards of each other. If you made it up for a drama, nobody would believe you. Once we were sure of this I felt a bit better about not being able to understand what was going on when it was put to me over the phone in the middle of the night.

So, we had to start investigating these crimes, particularly the robbery and then the robbery of the robbers. They'd sprayed CS gas in the face of the assistant in Cullens and then they'd tied him up with cable ties. He'd been able to give us a description of the duo, and from this we were sure they were the two men who had been shot in the Metro.

And we hadn't yet recovered a firearm...

This was 1994 and CCTV was much less advanced than it is these days. Across Liverpool Road from the Cullens branch was a pub which was a busy music venue and they had a CCTV system, albeit in black and white and recording to a VHS cassette. It was one where there were four cameras and the output went between them for two seconds at a time. Only one of those was of interest to us, and that was the external one, which they used to monitor queues outside the pub and showed the street.

It was the usual story – a VHS cassette that had been recorded on over and over, so many times that the quality had deteriorated. Everything was a two second jump – you had a frame we wanted, and then you've got three others and then it came back to the one we wanted. There was the potential there to try and work out what had happened, but it was going to be a long slog and a couple of officers were tasked to go through it.

We were able eventually to piece together from this very poor-quality footage the story of exactly what happened.

Through the CCTV footage, we had a view back up Liverpool Road where you could see the Cullens store on the right, Chapel Market and Marks & Spencer on the left, and the alley where the Metro was parked.

A group of men were there, loitering with the intention of robbing Cullens. They were waiting for their moment, they were waiting for staff to shut up shop, presumably to maximise their take, but also because at closing time there would be nobody else there. From the

CCTV, we could see they were waiting and watching, walking up and down and splitting into different groups and mingling again, trying to look innocuous. But they were ready to pounce and do the armed robbery.

Then, to their horror, two completely unknown men – Meek and Mullins – turned up and went in there to commit the exact same crime under their noses.

Mullins and Meek fled the scene, got back in the Metro to drive away, and the other gang made the instant decision: "We're going to go across the road and rob the robbers."

They shot Meek and Mullins, both of them, in the back of the neck. They then ran across with their own holdall, into which they had put the carrier bag and money, into Chapel Market. They were looking into the bag to see what they'd got away with when the police van came along, answering the alarm call to Marks & Spencer.

We never traced the two men who had broken into Marks & Spencer at the same time, but their actions were really helpful. Had they not set the alarm off at this store, then that van with the two uniformed constables wouldn't have come around the corner at exactly that point, wouldn't have seen the four men looking into the bag and running off, and so would never have arrested two of those men. I think there is a very good chance that all of them would have escaped. We'd have been left with a very difficult and long investigation trying to work out who it was who went across and shot Meek and Mullins.

The robbers saw the police van and scattered. They ran off in four different directions. And the police officers – who had no idea these were armed men who had just shot and left two men for dead – chased them bravely, arrested two and recovered the bag of money.

We hadn't recovered the firearm that had been used to shoot the two robbers, but we found it relatively quickly the next day as I had officers retrace the steps of the likely exit routes of the two men who hadn't been captured and found it discarded over a garden wall. It was a particularly unusual piece of equipment, a First World War British naval officer's revolver and it took a rather unusual size of ammunition which was almost obsolete.

But the cartridges did have a particular signature in terms of the chemicals that were used in them, the firearm residue that was left on these two men who had been shot was quite distinctive and the experts were able to match that up with the gun we'd found and confirm that it was almost certainly the ammunition used to shoot them.

We had two of the people in the cells, and we needed really to work on them, to find out who they were, and who their connections were.

They were Clifford Wilson and Joseph Brown, both from Northern Ireland. We interviewed them, and they "no commented" everything. We started doing some checks with Special Branch and found that both were known as being on the fringes of Protestant terror groups in the province.

The steer we were given was they were the sort of people who would commit crime – quite serious crime – and make a donation out of the proceeds. Or maybe they'd do a country house burglary, steal a shotgun, and give it to the terrorists. They weren't hardened terrorists, they were criminals who had sympathies with Protestant terrorism.

One of the men that was adrift still was somebody called Samuel Maclean, an associate of theirs who lived in south London, some way away from our normal patch.

He had fled down the escalator into the Angel tube station, and some pretty good quality colour CCTV had captured his image. Being of a fairly distinctive appearance – he's a gaunt man with a long ponytail – the investigation team were able to identify him.

We enlisted our local surveillance team to support us and go down to south London, perform surveillance on Samuel Maclean for a day, to see if he could lead us to exactly where he was living, but more importantly to anybody else he was associated with.

So, we went down to Brockley, it was the first time I'd been down to that part of the world really, to an old police station there and we had an early morning briefing. We waited, then went back to Islington. The team said it was the worst day of mobile surveillance they'd ever done in their lives. "What was the problem?"

The problem was that Samuel Maclean was a minicab driver and he was working. We didn't know that and the team spent the whole day following him taking fares to supermarkets and back and to hotel meetings and bingo halls. We didn't really find out until the very end where he lived. I got some friendly abuse from my colleagues for putting them behind a taxi all day because it was quite obviously a nightmare.

We then put some static surveillance on his address for a little while to see who came and went, and there was nobody noticeable, so he was then arrested and brought in as well.

They'd put the bag of money from Cullens into a holdall, and in that we found a part of a gun, but it wasn't a part of any gun from this offence. It looked like it was from a shotgun. It was sent to the lab, to see if they could make anything of it, and not only did we find a fingerprint on there for a man called Kenneth Macmillan, who was another associate of these men and was also from Northern Ireland, but the part was proved to have come from a firearm which had been recovered at an armed robbery, in February 1994 in west London – also at a Cullens store, where about £8,000 in cash was stolen. We couldn't prove Macmillan was the fourth man on the job at Islington, but we had an armed robbery for which he could be charged anyway so it was quite poetic all four of them were charged with armed robbery and serious offences.

Maclean, Wilson and Brown were each charged with the attempted murder of Meek and Mullins, as well as the armed robbery at Cullens. Kenneth Macmillan was charged with the west London Cullens robbery previously. We then started the normal kind of activity leading up to a trial, where we are trying to get the evidence in order, and trying to make sure we have the strongest possible case.

One of the difficulties we had was trying to make best use of this rather grainy, imprecise CCTV. A couple of the DCs on the team were looking at it, they spent eight or nine hours to try to work out what had gone on in a few minutes on the street. That was how difficult they had found it to interpret the images they had.

We knew that we had the CCTV footage and in terms of the quality of it, it was appalling. It was so bad. It was quadruplex – you had four cameras recording to one VHS tape in four parts, you've only got a quarter of the size of the screen for each one. It was a familiar story, they just recycled the tape and recorded over it and recorded over it again and again. The degradation in quality gets really bad, it was black and white, it was night time. And it was something we weren't used to using.

The James Bulger case in Liverpool was the first big case I remember CCTV being used for. We rang our friends in Merseyside to see if they can explain any sort of pitfalls how they went about it to use as evidence.

We had an office briefing and one of the DCs had produced what was almost a comic strip on a piece of paper with stick people. He was no artist, but he put these stick people on there in different frames and said: "This is the best we can work out exactly what happens." We looked at it and I just made one of these throwaway comments that sometimes inspire progress. "You should have drawn it on the corner of a telephone directory, so we could flick it through, and they'd move, like a moving picture we did as kids." There were a few chuckles about it.

I was then watching TV one evening and saw an advert for the new Channel Tunnel that had been made using computer animated images and I looked at that and thought: "If we could only do something like that but with these stickmen. So let's translate these stick men into a slick sort of computer animation that would enable us to present to the jury what that film was showing us."

The jury didn't have eight or nine hours to study the footage. If we put those grainy images up and somebody tried to explain it, they wouldn't see it straight away. It would be impossible to get over to them – in the time we had – the importance of what we were showing.

For much of the CCTV, you can't even work out that there's human beings on there. It's going to be so easy for the defence to say it showed nothing and the jury would agree. We needed to be able to show them what you can see if you slow it down and watch it carefully.

I kind of floated the idea past Doug Harvey, and he said he could see what I meant. I think he made a pretty good joke and said: "There'll be lots on the jury that are used to watching cartoons all day, it will probably go down well with them".

It was breaking new ground to a degree because nobody had ever done it before, as far as we were aware, I ran it past the CPS; their view was that if it was a qualified expert, if they were certain that what was in the animation was a representation of what was on the video, then it would admissible.

It was brilliant because it just showed so clearly what had happened and what had gone on. In some ways you needed that piece of evidence to prove that this ridiculously coincidental and outrageous set of circumstances had actually taken place.

I contacted a firm who did that sort of thing, they were down near Swindon, I went down with one of the officers. Commercial firms like that see that there is a potential opportunity to assist police in the future, and they even did it for us for nothing, saying: "We will do this as a trial to see if it works." We were allowed to use it, and I'm sure that was a very persuasive piece of evidence for the jury. They were able to sit and watch with absolute clarity what the CCTV had recorded.

All four men stood trial at the Old Bailey, and they all denied involvement. "It wasn't us, we weren't there." But we had the fingerprint evidence, and we also had the CCTV evidence which, with this animation, was easily presented to the jury.

Judge Michael Combs QC sentenced the men, and he remarked: "It's obvious you are ruthless men, utterly selfish, utterly determined to enrich yourselves no matter who might be hurt, physically or materially."

When you look at the sentences these men received, at the time they seemed about right. Certainly Macmillan, 12 years for one armed robbery seemed about right. The other three were sentenced really as if they'd committed a murder – they got 20 years.

These days, the aggravation of using a firearm means when you murder somebody with a firearm, the starting point is around 30 years, but that wasn't the case at the time. And the sentences were what we expected, and I think reflected the criminality and ruthlessness of the men.

Colin Meek – who to all intents and purposes made a full recovery from being shot in the neck with a reasonably big bore revolver slug – went back to life as before, and that life as before included committing armed robberies. He was eventually arrested by the Flying Squad, for a number of armed robberies in about 1997. They started to put a series of crimes to him, and one of them was the armed robbery at Cullens in Liverpool Road, Islington, at Easter 1994.

He said: "Yeah, I did do that, but I have this letter that says I can't be prosecuted for it." They looked at it and decided it probably wasn't legally valid and charged him with it anyway.

Almost inevitably, his defence team seized upon this and spoke to the CPS, and there was a degree of misremembering or amnesia there, because they didn't recall having the conversation with Doug Harvey and myself about the letter. I was summoned to go to the Old Bailey to go to Colin Meek's trial and was given a pretty tough time by his team in the witness box. I just told the truth and said: "This was the position, we spoke to the CPS, they told us to write the letter, we wrote the letter, he actually didn't tell us very much. He complied with his side of the deal, it's a matter for the court to decide what should be done about it."

And the decision of the court was that the letter shouldn't be a bar to prosecution, he was convicted of the Cullens robbery albeit several years later, and he was imprisoned for this and other armed robberies.

Upon his release he obviously decided to retire from armed robbery and in 2005, he finally got his own 20-year prison sentence, because he was convicted of a murder; the murder of a drug dealer who he shot while riding a motorbike. It was thought that it was a contract killing. Perhaps he thought that it was an easier way to make money than doing armed robberies. It was just another way for him to get into prison.

Gary Mullins on the other hand had been less lucky. The bullet, although it hadn't killed him, had severed his spinal cord at the neck, so he was quadriplegic from then onwards, it was a huge, life-changing injury.

He was eventually released from hospital and there was some sort of infamy I suppose, that he achieved when a national newspaper ran a story about Islington council spending a considerable amount of money – almost a million pounds – on equipping a bungalow for him. I think the thrust of that piece was that this man had got his injury while committing an armed robbery, yet the local council taxpayer was having to foot the bill for this converted house. But he was alive and needed to live, so the council had a duty to provide for him. He ended up needing all sorts of full-time care because of his condition and he died in a residential care facility in west London two or three years later.

Some of the criminals I've dealt with were maybe street smart – you could argue that Levi Bellfield was. But Meek and Mullins were definitely some of the more stupid robbers I've ever come across. They'd been involved in all sorts of low-level stuff for most of their teenage and young adult lives.

The very fact that they went to an armed robbery in a Metro, using that as a getaway car is quite amusing. And of course they didn't know what they were walking into. But nor did we. Remember that adage, detectives don't like coincidences. Until we knew it to be the case, nobody even suggested that it might have been two robbery gangs at work simultaneously, because, well, that just doesn't happen.

It was a really challenging investigation because it was one of those where you think you know where to start and then you start on it and you realise you don't know at all. And you've got to start all over again. It was good work by and large by lots of people.

Necessity is the mother of invention, as the old phrase goes. With this – and a couple of the others – it was a case of thinking: “How do we do it? How can we get around these problems and go from there to there?” If there was one thing I think I was good at, it was that kind of lateral thinking, thinking outside the box, thinking there must be a way to achieve this. And that was why I loved it when my officers did it on things like in the Bellfield case, to help identify the car and discovering the Tesco till rolls and recovering them and comparing the shopping list to our witnesses statement and crucially to prove the timing matched with what we already knew. When officers do things like that, I love it.

And that’s why I worry these days that police are so reliant on CCTV and DNA, that those sort of thinking skills will go from detectives and we will be up the creek without a paddle. It is a case of ‘this is the problem; this is what's stopping us being able to prove what we should be able to prove.’ When you find a solution to those problems that works, it's a good warm glow for everybody, you know you've achieved something.

CHAPTER 4

THE MURDER OF CHRISTOPHER DONOVAN

After the Cullens case, there were still no promotions in the Met. I applied for and got a job as DCI in West Yorkshire Police. I went up there to be a divisional DCI at a place called Eccles Hill which is north Bradford, it includes the towns of Baildon and Shipley. It was a wonderful new police station, but it was very, very different from London.

I moved there with the family – my son by then was coming up to four, my daughter was seven and a half. We bought a new house in a little village in the foothills of the Pennines, where there was space nearby for the horses and ponies that we seemed to have accumulated by then, as well as the dogs. I loved living in Yorkshire, I loved working in Yorkshire, it was with some really fantastic people. Had I not got divorced from my wife and she'd come back south, I'd probably have stayed there and everything would have been different, my career would have gone off in a completely different direction.

I'd been to university at Leeds from school, so I knew the area a bit. Before we went looking for houses, I don't think Maxine had been north of Cambridge in her life. The move was about having a nicer sort of area and lifestyle for my family, for the kids to grow up in, I thought it was nice to get them out of London. And it was a professional opportunity. It's something I'm really, really glad I did because I got so much from it.

When I eventually came back to the Met, it was because of personal circumstances rather than professional ones. I used to say that everybody should spend two years outside London in a county force because you just understand that the Met isn't the be all and end all of everything.

Nationally, West Yorkshire is quite a big force, but still much smaller than the Met. If you're a rural patrol officer out in the wilds of Todmorden or somewhere up in Calder Valley, you know that if you get out of the car and you're trying to do something, and you need help and support, then it's probably 20 minutes away, whereas if you're in the West End of London, you know that you've probably got somebody two minutes away. In that situation, you have to learn some pretty good interpersonal skills.

I got asked to manage a project about intelligence handling, which became the basis for the National Intelligence Model that was force-wide eventually and as a result of that I just got a phone call saying you're going to be head of Force Intelligence.

I once described this as like being head waiter at the Ivy – you'd be serving up all these wonderful dishes but you never actually got to taste them for yourself. I found it a bit frustrating because it was, for me, a bit too non-operational.

But while I was there, I had all the toys and technical support, bugging devices and secret cameras. This was during the late 1990s, early 2000s, when technology was making huge leaps and bounds almost on a daily basis. Every week I'd get my people at the technical support unit come up and say: "Boss we've got a man from so and so coming in to demonstrate a new piece of kit, do you want to come over?" They had a big hangar at headquarters where they did all this work – we had a covert entry team; I had a guy there who was a qualified master locksmith – he was actually a police officer and he'd go and work in a locksmith's in south London for two weeks every year to keep his accreditation up. He could break into places for us so we could put cameras in.

It was a really good place to be. The most important thing about it was that when I then came back to the Met, I had a really good appreciation of what covert policing could do, I was always willing and able to use covert techniques. Covert policing generally is mostly used in proactive work, mostly to combat serious drug dealers or armed robbers, it's not the first thing you think of when it comes to murder.

But actually, it was often used in murder cases, – they'd mic up a house like in the Stephen Lawrence case and then do something overt, like a search or arrest or even a media release, as a trigger to try and get people talking. There was also what used to be known as a talking table – a visitor table in a prison mic'd up and the prison staff would make sure that that's the table the target got to sit down at during a visit.

I was SIO for one decent case in West Yorkshire, it was a great story about a gang of Manchester armed robbers who had one of those little thin vans with the tiny wheels like a Suzuki Rascal. The reason they used them for armed robberies was that they could drive through narrow gaps that police cars couldn't get through. We used to have a morning meeting of the senior management team at half past nine every day. One morning I walked in at 29 minutes past nine as I normally did to see the Superintendent and the Chief Inspector of operations running. I asked what was going on, was there a fire or something? "No, it's an armed robbery across the road!"

This new police station was across the road from a little sort of shopping mall-type place, with a Morrisons, a furniture shop and one or two other bits and bobs. There were ATMs at the Morrisons and this gang had stuck up the men who were filling it up with £250,000. One of my DCs was off duty and in there doing his shopping with his shorts on. He appeared on the CCTV; people were asking why he didn't do anything. "What is he meant to do though?" I asked. "Throw his tin of beans at them?"

We worked out it was a Manchester crew from the van, we found it abandoned on our division and it was on false plates. When we looked at the vehicle identification (VIN) number it told us it had been stolen from Bury. I phoned the DCI in Greater Manchester Police's robbery squad and he told me he had a good idea who the gang were and added: "If you get any forensics off that van, I'll bare my arse on the town hall steps!" When we got the 17th fingerprint from inside it, I faxed him a map of Bradford; it had the town hall marked with a large, thick circle.

There had only been three men on the raid but we actually convicted four of the robbery, which was just a really good example of the absolute folly of lawyers sometimes. We've got this kid, he's 21 years old. He had stolen the van for them for a fee so they've given him something like 500 quid. He was given the instructions: "Go and nick us a van, put some false plates on it and bring it here." And that's what he did. But he managed somehow to leave his fingerprint on the back of one of the false plates and when we had it examined it betrayed who he was. My team went in to interview him and came out telling me he was going solidly "no comment". I sat with his solicitor and said: "Look, if he says no comment, he's getting charged as being part of the robbery team. If he confesses that he was paid to steal the van and give it to them, he gets charged with stealing the van."

Next interview there was no change: "No comment, no comment."

He got charged with robbery, sentenced to four and a half years' imprisonment and he wasn't even on the job.

Essentially, it was a bad idea to move to Yorkshire as far as Maxine was concerned. She didn't settle down anywhere. I started applying for jobs back south, but didn't manage to get one. By the time we got to 2000, she just really wanted to go back, so she went to stay with her dad and I stayed in Yorkshire. By the time I did get a job back in Surrey she'd actually realised she quite liked it that way around.

Later in 2000, I finally got a job in Surrey. I hated it. I just didn't like the way Surrey was run. It was too quiet. I was working on the implementation of the National Intelligence Model in Guildford Police Station and living in my soon to be ex-mother-in-law's flat in Surbiton, because she was away teaching in Greece. I then rented a flat in Bookham, in Surrey, so I was living close to the kids, you know.

There was only one murder case that came to me in Surrey.

Christopher Donovan was by all accounts an ordinary, nice, sensible young lad of 18, growing up ready to make his way into the world. He came from a family who were very committed Christians, his mother and father, Ray and Vi, were regular churchgoers. They had a daughter as well as two boys and it was a close family.

Chris had been a model son and he had this ambition, after he got a little bit older, of becoming a policeman. One fateful night, he'd been working at a pizza shop at Tolworth and his brother, Philip, and a friend, Richard, met him there. They were just walking home, in high spirits – they were singing and talking to each other, they weren't drunk, they were just walking home together.

And as Jack Regan, the Surrey Police Detective Sergeant I worked with on the case and formed a good team with, said: "Out of the blue, for some reason, nobody knows exactly why, an incident sparked where a group attacked them".

Chris' parents were woken up by police in the middle of the night. As Ray Donovan said: "They said that Chris had been involved in a fight, he is seriously injured, and we need to get to Epsom hospital straight away.

"When we got there Philip and his friend Richard were in forensic clothing, Philip's face was all blooded, as I'm talking to Phil, another policeman came up and said, 'you can't see Chris they're operating on him'."

He continued: "Then at 20 to four in the morning, we'd seen the doctors, the police, the hospital chaplain. They didn't have to tell us, their faces told us, Christopher died that morning, because one 15-year-old coward wanted respect from his friends."

I found out about the case the morning after it had happened, it was a weekend in May and I actually had the following week booked off for leave – I was meant to be going on holiday for a week. It was half term. I had a little boat on the Thames and we were going to go away on the boat with the kids. I still believe to this day, the only reason they actually let me investigate a murder, which no-one ever did, was because everybody else was on leave and it was school holidays. But you know, needs must, and they didn't have anybody else who could run the investigation.

I was asked by the assistant chief constable to be the SIO for this murder and he told me that an 18-year-old lad had been murdered on the Ewell bypass on the previous night. The incident room was at Epsom Police Station, so I had to go there and meet the people who would be on my team.

There wasn't a permanent murder squad in Surrey at that time. What happened was that you were appointed SIO and then you were given sufficient staff that were selected from various divisions. I turned up in Epsom and found that the acting DI, the DS who was going to be my number two, was the aforementioned Jack Regan, I'd never met him before but he was one of these people I just instantly took to. He was a very different character to me, probably a bit more sparky and a bit more expressive. I think it was one of those situations where we had two people whose qualities complement each other, and together, we made a good team, and it was great working with him.

This murder really was all about two groups of young people. You had one group – mostly young men but one or two women – and they'd been at a party at a flat above the shops at the Ewell bypass on the A240. They'd left the party and were walking towards Tolworth to go home; most of them lived on the Watersedge Estate so they'd go up the A240 and turn left towards it. They crossed the road and started to walk down the same side as Chris, his friend and brother.

The group from the party had all been taking drugs, amphetamines, and they'd been drinking. Chris had just finished work, he was walking home and his group of three were all sober. These two groups didn't know each other, there was nothing pre-arranged, there was no history between the groups, it was something that happened on the spur of the moment as they bumped into each other on the street.

And then some sort of argument started. It might have been about singing the words to a song wrong, something as simple as that. It might have been banter. But there was an altercation and for whatever reason these two groups of youths started arguing. The argument turned into a fight.

The problem was, those who had come from the party had not only been drinking but taking drugs as well; how much that clouded their judgement we can't really say, but the fight happened.

The location was bordered on both sides of the road – it was a dual carriageway, but there were houses on both sides. It was around midnight on a Friday night. The fight went on for some minutes and there was loud shouting. It went on for so long that people in their houses heard it. Some of them went to their bedroom windows, looking out of their windows at the fighting youths. Some went to see what was going on, which was very helpful for us as the investigation went on.

What they did see was this group of young people milling about, fighting each other. During the fight Chris Donovan was knocked unconscious, he fell to the ground, and while he was there, lying prone, someone kicked him hard in the head. While he was unconscious, lying in the roadway, a poor woman at the traffic lights pulled away in her car, drove up the hill and saw what she thought was a bin bag or a bundle of rags in the road. There was another vehicle close to her, so she tried to straddle it with her wheels.

It wasn't a bundle of rags, it was Chris Donovan. Part of his clothing got caught on the exhaust as the car passed over him and he was dragged him along the road for 70-80 feet before the driver realised and stopped. This added to the injuries Chris had suffered – as well as the head injury that caused him to be unconscious, he also had terrible abrasion injuries across his body from the road. This poor woman was destroyed, it wasn't her fault it could have happened to anybody.

There was a lot going on the first morning after the murder.

Obviously we treated the blameless driver as a witness, not as a suspect. But we had to seize her car, so we could examine it.

We had traced a number of eye witnesses, which was somewhat out of the ordinary. They were able to tell us exactly what they had seen happening, and who was doing what. This would become incredibly helpful as the investigation went on.

We also got a lot of calls into the incident room, it was most unusual to get a murder in Ewell and people in the community wanted to help. It didn't take long for people at the Watersedge Estate to start calling in, giving us the names of the youths that they had heard were in the assailant gang. We had a range of youths from 15 years old to their early 20s. It was one of those situations where names were repeated, different people calling in with the same names and so we began to take the calls seriously and research these as suspects.

The overnight team went out to make arrests. You might think it's useful to have people arrested, often it is. But it can be a double-edged sword. When they're under arrest their custody clock is ticking away, you can only keep them a certain time. If you've not got any evidence that's going to lead you to be able to charge them and they're not talking to you or telling you what happened, then it can create as many problems as it solves. That was the situation we were in, we had all these people there, we could interview them and get an account if they would talk to us.

But ultimately they'd have to be released on bail and we would have to carry on the investigation until we found the evidence to justify their re-arrest.

We knew the eyewitnesses were going to be important, and when we started speaking to them and getting their statements, what we found was of course they didn't know who they were talking about. But they could remember clothing. They were saying things like "oh, I saw the lad who was wearing a pink polo shirt with a big blue number two on the back punch somebody… I saw the boy with the light trousers and the blue top kick somebody". We had all these accounts of people wearing clothing doing things rather than names, so it was going to become important early on to establish who was wearing what on the night. It was the way we were going to make these eye witness accounts work for us as evidence.

It was the key to convicting the ones who did it, because by proving a line from an individual's clothing to what a witness had said we could piece a case together. I had no illusions that it would be easy and we had to hope they'd not thrown the clothing away or swapped clothes about as groups of young people do.

And we had to present it all in a logical and coherent way, one which would convince the CPS lawyers if they were to support our charging them and, ultimately, persuade a jury in court.

We also had to try to prove what had killed him. Was it the impact with the car and being dragged along the road? Or was it the assault? Legally speaking, if you knock someone out and leave them in the road and they get run over, you're still liable for it. But it would be a lot easier to prove the causation if it could be established that the assault had killed Chris. It was a short post-mortem examination. It was 2001, before we were spending seven to eight hours doing one because there wasn't an ability to take DNA from virtually anything as there is these days.

The injuries that Chris suffered were quite extensive and the pathologist was a doctor called Ashley Fegan-Earl, he was very helpful in the sense that he was quite categorical about what he said. He examined every inch of Chris's body and he was able to say quite definitely that the injuries he suffered from the neck upwards were from the assault and the injuries from the neck down were from abrasion, from being dragged along under the car.

So, even though the car was involved, it really was of no consequence. We were only really looking at proving the assault – who hit or kicked Chris in the head.

One of the things that came out of the post-mortem was that Chris had quite short hair, which was shaved further so that we could see any injuries more clearly. On the top of his scalp, there was a quite well-defined pattern of bruising and it looked for the world as if it were a print from some sort of ridged sole, from a training shoe or some similar footwear.

It looked like somebody stamped down right on the very top of his head, and this confused us. It was difficult to imagine the circumstances where somebody could get in that position to stamp on his head. Maybe if he had been climbing out of a manhole then you could do it. But in the fight, from the eye-witness accounts we had, we had no idea how that could have happened.

It is quite a simple method we use to find a match for this kind of print. We'd put a pair of training shoes onto a photocopier and press the button. We could then take the photocopy of the sole and compare it to the marks. But when we got the clothing and training shoes from all the people that had been arrested and started looking at them, there wasn't a pair of shoes or pair of trainers that came anywhere close to matching this mark on Chris's head.

It troubled me for a few days. It was obvious that the mark was bruising and definitely something to do with the assault. But it didn't look like someone could have left it by stamping. I went back to the mortuary with Jack Regan two or three days after the post-mortem and asked the mortuary attendant to let us have another look at Chris's head. In my experience, bruising can sometimes get darker and be more distinctive after a few days have passed, so I wanted another look.

We looked at it and it was almost like doing one of those Magic Eye puzzles that used to be in the newspapers where you sort of squint and half-look and something appears. And it became obvious what the mark was. It wasn't from the sole of a shoe. It was from the in-step. It was the mark of where the laces have been crossed across the in-step, side to side above the tongue. It tied in perfectly with one of the witnesses who described seeing somebody kick Chris "like a penalty kick". It makes much more sense that if he's on the floor, then a kick like that would easily land on the scalp on top of his head.

The difficulty with this was the way that your trainers are laced up can vary each time, it also depends on whether there's a foot in there and the thickness of any socks. It wasn't possible conclusively to compare the mark on Chris's head with any one of the shoes we had.

The witnesses from nearby houses were very good in that they were able to tell us what individual people were doing and they'd seen someone wearing a certain item of clothing punching or kicking or whatever, but of course they didn't know the actual identity of these people. That's where the investigation had to go, to find out who the person with the pink polo shirt with the number two on the back was, who the person with the white hooped top on was.

What we needed to do was to try and prove our suspects were there and they were wearing the clothing that the witnesses described. We went back to looking for CCTV. Bear in mind that it was 2001 – CCTV wasn't nearly as good as it is now. But even so we found some good images, one of them was on a garage in Tolworth that had a camera that pointed out at right angles straight across the road. We used the logic that if the assailant group walked back towards that garage from the party, if we went back far enough on the CCTV, we would probably see them going to the party and they'd still be wearing the same clothes. It proved to be some of the best evidence, when they were all together walking past that camera down the hill towards the party at the shops earlier in the evening.

We also found out from someone who phoned the incident room that two of them had gone by train to Clapham Junction, south London, to score some drugs for the party. We went to British Rail for CCTV and sure enough we were able to see two of our suspects – wearing the clothes that witnesses described – going from Stoneleigh Station towards Clapham Junction and later coming back with their drugs and going to the party.

Another key location was the off-licence opposite where the party took place, where the assailant group had gone to buy drinks before the party. It was useful because the lighting conditions indoors meant some of the images we got there were the clearest; they unmistakably showed the clothing the people were wearing at the time.

Using the CCTV, we were able to piece together the items of clothing the assailants were wearing and that's how we made a case against the three men who eventually stood trial. We were able to really work out exactly what everyone was wearing because, fortunately for us, they were all very distinguishable, people who had similar colour shirts on had different colour trousers on and so on. They were all quite distinctive.

When we had the CCTV evidence, they were re-arrested and they started talking to us to a degree but each of them was saying similar things: "Yes I was there, but I wasn't involved, I didn't throw any punches, I didn't throw any kicks". We put together a matrix, like a spreadsheet of all the witnesses across the top and down the side, the clothing they'd been seen with, what they saw that person wearing that clothing doing. So, witnesses would say: "Pink shirt punched somebody, blue-hooped shirt kicked somebody, plain blue shirt kicked and punched somebody."

The problem that I foresaw was that trying to express that to a jury in terms of giving them a spreadsheet with crosses and ticks was just going to be very technical and dry; it would be difficult to convince them. But first we had to be sure ourselves that we knew who was wearing what and what they did.

We were talking about how we could present what we'd found and what we knew to the judge and jury, because it's difficult to convey the contents of a spreadsheet succinctly for a jury to understand. We were talking over it and Jack Regan made a throwaway comment: "What we need to do is dress half a dozen mannequins and let the jury see it." He was talking about it theoretically, but I took it literally and said it was a fantastic idea, we should borrow some tailor's dummies, put the real clothes we have seized from the suspects onto those mannequins, put them in the same locations under the same lighting conditions with the same cameras from which we had seized the CCTV images. We could then say to the jury: "Compare the CCTV to the pictures we've taken' and that's how you get it over to them."

We went to a local well-known clothing and food store in Epsom and they lent us six of their best brand-new mannequins. We got the clothing we'd seized from the suspects and we dressed each of the mannequins in what we believed, from the witnesses, each suspect had been wearing that night.

So it was clear who we were saying who the suspect was, we had a name plate on each dummy. A police photographer took photos of the mannequins and then we put the them into a police minibus, drove down to the Ewell bypass and took with us still photo prints from the garage, rail station and off licence. We posed the mannequins in exactly the same spots, facing the same way, with the same order of people with the same clothes on, exactly as the prints showed us they had been on the night of the murder. We let the CCTV film it again and took a still from there so we had as much as we could – identical lighting, equipment and clothing.

When you compared the two pictures – one of the real people and our new one with the mannequins – it was startling that they were so alike; all the differences in colour and lighting were eliminated by the process because we had the same equipment and same lighting conditions. It would be crystal clear to the jury – we could just give them both versions and say: "Here's the CCTV, there's the same clothes and here's who we seized it from and that's how we can tell who is who." It was a novel, slightly off the wall idea but it worked fantastically well.

It was a crucial part of our success, undoubtedly the best way to present it to a jury because we had the witnesses saying "I saw people wearing these clothes doing these things" and that would convict them if the jury could be sure to whom the witness was referring. We had to make the jury understand who was wearing those clothes and to have no doubt about it. By having the ability to compare the clothes we seized from an individual with how they looked under the same cameras on the same night then they could make the link, they could be certain that that person was wearing those clothes on that night and thereafter that three witnesses saw him kick the victim.

We didn't do this exercise with the mannequins before we sent the clothing away to be examined because obviously it was more important to preserve any fibres or blood or any other evidence that might be on these clothes. The only thing that came up was there was a black jacket which belonged to one man, but he had lent it to another young man who was wearing it at the time - they had told us this. There was a speck of blood on the sleeve. The lad who was wearing the jacket admitted he punched someone, but he said he punched Philip, Chris' brother, during the melee. He said he didn't punch Chris, the man who died.

One interesting element of the discussions showed the relationship Jack Regan and I had. We went to a conference with the QC who was going to be leading the prosecution. He was of the view that we shouldn't proceed with the case against the one with the speck of blood on the sleeve of his jacket, because it related to the brother and not the victim. Jack made an impassioned plea to the lawyer along the lines of "no, we've got them". It was all very dramatic.

Jack finished his monologue and I took a more considered line; I tried to make it more logical. "We can prove he was there and we can prove that the blood means he punched somebody. It's a joint enterprise in the fight, he punches someone and Chris dies, even if it's someone else he punched, he's still a murderer." The barrister saw my argument right away and conceded, agreeing to leave him in. That individual was convicted of murder under the joint enterprise rule.

The trial at the Old Bailey took place in March/April 2002, 10 months after the offence. The judge heard applications from counsel for the youngest defendant, asking that he be allowed to sit in the well of the court rather than the dock. The argument from the defence was that his age and inexperience meant the proceedings could be explained to him by a solicitor sitting next to him. It would mean he could have access to his lawyer at all times and understand what was going on. We thought this was obviously a ploy to try separate him from the older men in the dock, to put some distance between him and the others and to try and put it all on them.

The judge thought about the application overnight and his ruling the following morning was well-considered. It also came as something of a shock both to us and especially I think to the lawyer who made the application. For the judge said that while he accepted that the youngest defendant might need to be treated differently, it might be prejudicial to his co-defendants if he were separated from them. His solution was to require the instructing solicitor or a representative of them to sit in the dock with the defendant for the entire trial, and also that the young defendant and his lawyers must stay behind for half an hour after the court had risen each afternoon, so that the day's proceedings could be debriefed for him.

It was surprising and I'd certainly never before encountered a case where a judge has required a legal representative to sit in the dock with a client the whole time. I do wonder sometimes if the lawyer ever dared make a similar application in the future.

Throughout the trial, the defendants were saying it was nothing to do with them individually, and while they weren't exactly pointing their fingers at their friends, it was always there, unsaid, in the background. They were, in effect, saying: "I was there but I didn't do anything, it was other people."

It didn't matter ultimately, it was a joint enterprise. They were all convicted of murder. The youngest of the defendants was given a recommendation of serving only six years of his life sentence. I think the minor role he played was reflected in the recommendation given by the judge.

There were elements of old-fashioned and modern detection in the investigation. Using witness statements and eyewitnesses is something you hope to do, but it became increasingly difficult throughout my service. We had got to a stage where the public were most reluctant to put themselves forward as witnesses. This was a case where people did, but then you've got the forensics of being able to find a speck of blood and match that to an individual as well as the CCTV. In terms of the investigation it was a mixture, a hybrid.

The big thing for me was this crazy thing with the mannequins, I still think it probably helped us make sure the case got over the line.

The remarkable thing about the Donovan family, his parents Ray and Vi Donovan, is how they reacted to their son's death. I felt rather hopeless when we got a guilty verdict. I was in the courtroom at the Old Bailey when we got it and we all went to meet upstairs in the canteen.

Ray and Vi came across and it was very tearful; tears of joy and relief. We hugged and they said: "Come on, we're taking you for a drink."

I thought: "When I wake up tomorrow, I'm going to be going back to work and taking on a new case. When they wake up tomorrow, it's over."

Just imagine them having in their head this hurdle of the trial coming up and getting the guilty verdict. You get it, what now? I felt really powerless and almost insignificant at that point.

We had done the best we could and this was the best result we could hope for. But the next morning, they've still lost their son. That's why I always say closure doesn't exist because people just learn to manage and to live with the fact that they lost a loved one to murder.

Vi and Ray are both committed Christians and they looked at the tragedy, looked at the terrible situation that they were in and thought: "How can we make the best of this? How can we turn this to a force for good?" And with the Christopher Donovan Trust they launched, that's exactly what they did.

They go around to prisons, they go to schools and talk about restorative justice, they talk to people, to young people about their lives and how they shouldn't waste them. I've met people, young men they have spoken to who have told me: "If it weren't for Ray and Vi Donovan's work, I would either be in prison or I would be dead."

They really have made a force for good out of the tragedy that was the murder of their son.

And of course, Ray and Vi found it by turning a huge negative into a positive, they're amazing people. There's never any right or wrong way to react. It's how they reacted and how they've dealt with it. And it's worked for them and in doing so, they've actually done a lot of good for other people.

It reminds you why you do these things. I have met more recently bereaved people than almost anybody, other than perhaps undertakers. Sometimes the way that meeting and the kind of ongoing relationship goes means that there's something bit more there. I'm still in touch with Amelie Delagrange's parents. It's difficult because we haven't got the language. I don't do any French, and they don't really do much English, but I get my daughter, who did French at university to translate.

Sometimes you get that relationship but it's not a question of looking for it. I didn't feel I had to become friends with every single family that I came across. But if it happened naturally and organically, like it did with them, then it happens.

It wasn't the first case I lead as SIO, but it was the first substantial one; the first I did where I understood and realised then how important it was for me to be visible to the victim's family and for me to inspire confidence in them. I wanted to give them a certain amount of comfort. I said to them: "I'm not going to promise you we'll get them because I can't. But I promise you we'll do absolutely everything we can."

There's no good promising people things which are out of your control. You never know if the investigation going to work out or not. Sometimes the evidence simply can't be found; it is rare but it does happen.

But it was more about silly little things. Ray Donovan always remembers the fact that I asked him for a photo because we were going to do an appeal for witnesses. They gave the photo and he said it was the last decent photo they had of him. So when I gave it to our media people, I asked if they could make me a dozen or so copies. I took them and I gave them to Ray and Vi. He's remembered that to this day, he mentions it every time I see him. It's just little things like that; nobody ever taught me to do that. It was just something that I thought of at the time, that it would be nice to do it for them.

It's quite a dehumanising process and I wanted to be the opposite. To show that we cared, and I took the experience from Chris's murder forward into every subsequent investigation I led. I always say that to the Donovans that I learned a lot from them.

One of those charged was meant to be joining the army soon after he was arrested. He got life in prison, but with a recommendation he serve eight years because of his age. Before he was released from prison, when I was back in the Met, maybe two or three years later, I was driving home down the A3, the traffic as usual was terrible. I was sitting in traffic, listening to the radio. And I realised there was a Ford Escort van, next to me in the queue. I recognised the driver – it was this youngster's dad. As I looked at him, he looked at me and he'd obviously seen me as well. The window came down. My heart sank, I thought I can't deal with this and the traffic.

"Hello Mr Sutton, how are you?"

I asked how his son was.

"He's doing well, he's doing well, he's doing okay. He's growing up."

He went on. "Hey, look," he said, "it could have been worse. He could have been out in Afghanistan, couldn't he?"

"Well, that's one way of looking at it."

"No," he said, "you know, as I said to you at the time, Mr. Sutton, he did the wrong thing. He's got to pay for it."

When I first started that conversation, when I saw him put his window down, I thought: "Oh no, this is going to be uncomfortable."

You've got a father there and you put his 16-year-old son away for murder. But we had a reasonable conversation and I thought to myself: "Do you know what, we must have been doing the job at least half-right."

It would have been so easy for him to feel bitter and twisted.

If we can leave the parents of our murderers with that sort of attitude towards the way we do our job, then we must be doing it properly.

CHAPTER 5
THE MURDER OF BRIDGET 'BRIDIE' SKEHAN

When I joined the police, I had no idea what specialism I wanted to do, I just thought, you know, I wanted to be a policeman; I wanted to be in uniform and run around chasing people and driving after people, catching criminals and helping people, and all the other things you do.

What I did know – or thought I knew – is that I didn't want to be a detective. It all kind of changed the very first time I went into a room where there was a murder squad in operation. I just thought 'that's actually a really good job, I quite fancy doing that!'. It was just a hopeless dream at the time, I never thought it would actually happen. I was on a different career path completely which meant a quick promotion to at least inspector and working in uniform. And I did all that.

Then I got the chance to be a detective and I took it.

But the more I worked in Surrey, the keener I was to get back in the Met. It happened by chance really. They used to run this exercise for senior investigating officers and others called Critical Incident weekends, a national training program, I was a Surrey officer but there were a lot of others there. One of those was George Rhoden, chair of the Black Police Association. He came from Enfield, and in the mid or late 70s, he was the butchery boy at the Co-op in Enfield Town when I was the delicatessen boy. We had a sort of shared appreciation of the same type of music. so I'd see him around quite a bit. We met locally and then he joined the police before me.

It was quite late, I was in the bar, catching up with George and there was a senior officer there called Bill Griffiths who was Deputy Assistant Commissioner who was running the whole exercise. And he said something to me along the lines of: "What are you doing fucking about in Surrey then?" I told him the Met wouldn't have me; they had told me there were no DCI vacancies when I had tried to return from West Yorkshire. He just told me to write him a letter; the Met was not actually advertising. I spoke to an ex-Met officer in Surrey and he advised me to apply for an SIO post on Operation Trident, the Met squad dealing with murders within the black community. His reasoning was that fewer people wanted those jobs so I would have less competition. So I wrote a letter and I got an interview to come back to the Met, chaired by a Trident Detective Superintendent named John Sweeney.

By now it was the middle of 2002. Mr Sweeney was talking about Trident and how it would mean a huge increase in workload for me, something like 20 to 24 new investigations a year, compared to just over one a year in Surrey Police.

"Well, how do you feel about that? You know, that's a huge increase in workload…"

"I think it's great. I said, bring it on. Love it."

"Really? Why would you want that?"

"Well, if you've only got... one or two jobs a year and you cock it up, you've got no excuse. If you've got 24, you've got all the excuse in the world."

John Sweeney phoned me later that evening. By now he said he'd been thinking about my answer and still thought it was a bit of a jump. I confided in him that I didn't really want to do Trident, but had been advised that to apply for it would boost my chances.

He replied: "If you don't want to do that, we'll just put you down for an ordinary murder team."

I said: "Well, that's what I really want."

"OK, great, no problem. You've got the job then."

And that was that.

They said they had a job for me in west London, but it wouldn't be available until January 2003, but if I'd like to come in September 2002, they could use me on the murder review team. It got me out of Surrey more quickly and also, as I'd been out of the Met for six years, I thought it would give me a good chance to reacclimatise without it being too risky because I wouldn't actually be doing live new murders. So I ended up doing the Murder Review Group which was interesting because it was all looking at cold cases. A lot of it was administrative. It was looking at the database, more of a case of looking to make sure you hadn't done anything wrong, rather than looking to solve the crime.

It was a little bit frustrating, but I quite enjoyed it. I was living in Surrey at Woking and my first posting was to Shooters Hill. I had to drive from Woking to south east London, which really was not good. And then I went to Woodford – I used to go in like for an early turn, I'd get up about half five, get in the car, and I'd get over to Woodford by about seven, seven thirty depending on the traffic. I'd drive straight through the middle of London, straight up through the A4, in through the middle of London back out to Woodford. And then I'd do my eight hours, and because I didn't have to do overtime or anything like that being on the review team, I'd drive home around the M25. I'd occasionally stay with my parents in Enfield. I liked working over that way again, it was near my old stomping ground.

And then on January 3 2003 I took over the team at Barnes. I was looking forward to getting down there and actually being an SIO, meeting the murder team for the first time.

I'd got married again in 2002. Louise was the Principal Analyst in Surrey Police. We knew each other already, she'd worked in West Yorkshire and we'd bumped into each other at a conference when she was working in Kent. On New Year's Eve 2002 into 2003, just before I went to Barnes, we were going to my parents in Enfield. We were coming along on the A10 and Louise said, we've got to go and take some wine or something nice. We stopped at the Morrisons in Enfield. We're just about to go in and there's like a conservatory on the end where you come out; there were sliding automatic doors on the side of it. We were by those doors as a young black lad came out with a longish knife in one hand and a bottle of Moet in the other – with a Morrisons employee grabbing onto each of his limbs.

I thought that doesn't look too clever. I didn't know if this would work but I thought let's not allow him out, so I grabbed the automatic sliding doors and held them shut. It was a success, the doors stayed shut and he couldn't get out. More staff caught up with him and they got him to the floor. I then realised Louise had gone through the door while they were open and she was inside. Once they had got him subdued, I let the doors open, went in and introduced myself to these two security guards and two other members of staff. They said: "Right, let's get him up".

I said: "No, don't get him up. My wife's phoned 999. Just leave him where he is for now and send everybody out through those other doors."

So we left him there, and just to make sure I knelt on him a bit. We got the knife off him as well as the bottle of champagne. We were waiting for the sirens, then you heard them coming.

There's no threat now. Louise was a special in West Yorkshire, so although she was worked for the police as a civilian, she knew the procedures. And she nudged me and said: "He's not breathing too well." He didn't sound too clever. I said: "What do you want mate?"

"Asthma."

He had an asthma inhaler in his pocket, I got it and gave it to him while he was down the floor. She said: "You could have killed him, you know, positional asphyxia?" Thank God she was watching.

And so, on the third day of the new year, I was on my first day with my new murder team at Barnes in south west London on the western part of the homicide and serious crime command.

Although I had been SIO on a few other cases when I was serving with other forces, this was the first time I had a team dedicated to only doing serious crime all the time and I knew in that respect most of my team had more experience than I did. It was something I approached with a little bit of apprehension, I wanted to make sure that I did it well and that I could prove to the team that they could trust me, just the same as I was going to have to watch them to see if I could trust them.

I went in that day and was introducing myself to the members of the team, chatting to them and they were talking me through a few of the current outstanding investigations. About half past one in the afternoon I got a phone call from the main office for the homicide group and they said: "Your team is now in the frame".

This meant that when there is a new investigation in the area, and we would be the team to take it on and pick it up. At about 4pm I got the call: "There might be a job in Paddington near Marble Arch, there's a 92-year-old woman reported missing since Boxing Day – just over a week – and we're fearing the worst now. She may have been brought to some harm, so can you take your team down there to have a look."

I didn't have time to sit down and talk to each one of the officers and find out what they thought about things and how they worked. I had just about moved my things into the office, and we were out on a job. It was a funny sort of situation that day because we were quite literally thrown in at the deep end. But it gave me an opportunity to see most of the members of my team in action for real, it was really just what I needed at the very start of my career with my new group.

I suppose in some ways I didn't really know how best to deal with it. Do I send somebody to have a look and report back to me? What would they be expecting me to do? I thought it wouldn't really do any harm if I'm there can it? If I'm there making decisions on the scene, it's probably the best way to do it, I grabbed a handful of officers and we went to take a look.

We went down to Lanchester Court and met the local police and a local DI, who told us this woman was Bridie Skehan. She was a colourful and interesting character, she'd had quite a life.

During the Second World War, she had worked at the American Embassy and after that she became an interior designer. She had a love for big, ostentatious American cars. She led a life with the party-set and money-set in London and was something of a socialite, a celebrity before there really was such a thing. Bridie had been married at some point in her life, but it didn't work out – she was divorced, and she had lived alone for many years.

Now in her 90s, she had a flat and rented out rooms in it to lodgers. One of the lodgers came back from Christmas with his family while we were in the premises and he started talking to us. He said Bridie had last been seen by Molly, her neighbour, who lived opposite. She had been missing for about a week and obviously with her age, 92, you can understand why the local police and indeed her lodger and Molly, her friend, were fearful for her safety.

We got talking to them and they told us there were two other lodgers, a couple, a Filipino woman and a Middle Eastern man who weren't there, although they should have been – they were meant to be staying in the flat all over Christmas.

We were having sort of a cursory look around the flat and there was nothing obviously amiss, no signs of a struggle or anything that would have raised alarm bells. But the lodger was sort of scratching his head and looking around with us.

And I saw his gaze fell upon on some hooks in the kitchen. It was clear that there was something that caught his eye. "What's wrong, what's the matter?" I asked.

He said there was a key to the shed of the flat that ought to have been hanging on a hook in the kitchen and it was missing.

I kind of looked at the local DI and he looked at me and we sort of shrugged our shoulders, we weren't aware that this flat had a shed which went with it. The lodger explained that if you go out to the street and to the end of the block, there was an archway that took you to the service alley round behind the block of flats and there were out-houses. They weren't very big but some of the flats had one allocated to them. Bridie's flat was one of those.

By this time, the weather had become quite foul and it was snowing really, really heavily. Given that the key was missing, and we now knew there was another part of the premises that hadn't been searched, we thought we better go around and do it.

We went back out to the street, walked around the building and ended up in the alley behind Lanchester Court. It was thick with snow. We went to the shed – a brick-built building, quite small about 8 by 6 feet – and of course it was locked, and we didn't have the key.

DC Dave Leach obliged by putting his shoulder to the door and it didn't give much resistance. We looked inside by torchlight. Our attention was immediately drawn to this large cardboard box at the far end of this small space – it was a box a TV had been delivered in. We could see that it wasn't sort of buried, it was sitting prominently and it was the first thing that caught your eye.

Then, when you looked at it more closely, it was clear that in a corner at the bottom, there was a quadrant that looked like it was damp and that looked pretty ominous to all of us. Why would there be something in there leaking fluids? It was a dark brown, red colour. Blood staining.

I looked at Dave who was a trained exhibits officer. He said: "I'd better go get kitted out." He went and put a forensic suit on, a paper suit and mask. I was standing outside the shed with a few other officers and Dave was good because he gave a commentary of what he was doing; he was an experienced officer doing the right thing. So he announced that what he was going to do was take a scalpel and cut away a piece of the dark quadrant in the corner and see what was behind it.

He took some care in cutting into this cardboard box, he was very gentle and didn't push his scalpel any further than he needed to, because he didn't want to disturb anything. He took out a large sized chunk of cardboard, cut it away and then shone his torch on the hole.

The first thing you could see looked like it was artificial grey, silver fur, sort of long strands of silver hair. Behind it was this dark pink surface. It was obvious right away that we had found Bridie. She was in a cardboard box.

The last time Bridie was seen was when she went with Molly, her friend from the adjacent flat, to midnight mass at Westminster Cathedral; they'd walked back from the service together.

She was reported missing in between Christmas and New Year by Molly and we had now got to January 3, so it was getting on to 10 days since Bridie had last been seen.

One of the things that the neighbour Molly was able to tell us was something about what was going on in the flat prior to Christmas. Bridie supplemented her pretty low income by having lodgers in her big flat with her. She lived in her flat with a lodger who was a lawyer, another lodger who was an accountant and then she had two other lodgers who were kind of a couple and they'd been there for a few months. The woman was called Nympha Ong and the man was called Ahmed Al Haddad.

It was a four-bedroom flat, the lawyer lived in one bedroom, the accountant in another and in theory, Ong and Al Haddad had a bedroom each, but what was really happening was that the couple were mostly always sharing a bed, or sharing a bedroom. And this kind of upset Bridie because of her morality and she didn't want two unmarried people living under her roof. In fact, Bridie who owned the flat, had, because of this taken to sleeping on the sofa in the living room. And they'd had words about it and ultimately, Bridie had asked them to leave the flat and not to come back to it after Christmas.

Everybody had disappeared from the flat, there was nobody, none of the lodgers was there. They'd gone back home for Christmas but likewise, Al Haddad and Ong were not there. They should have been, they were meant to have been living there until the end of December. Immediately, they were our prime suspects, we had to try and find Nympha Ong and Ahmed Al Haddad.

We had also found out that Al Haddad had a brother who lived nearby in Harrowby Street, on the other side of Edgware Road, near Marylebone. We went there to see if he was in, to see if that might have been the place Al Haddad had fled to. We knocked on the door and got no reply. But by this time it was 1.30am or so, mainly because of all the forensic and intelligence work we'd done. I was really of the view that perhaps we ought to go home, get some rest and be fresh in the morning.

We were just by the police car organising that and a man came around the corner. One of the officers noted: "That bloke there looks a bit like Al Haddad." It was a bit of a stretch really, a bit of a punt, but he went over to him and said: "Are you Ahmed Al Haddad?"

The man replied: "No, I'm not, I'm his brother, but he is just behind me."

And there was our suspect just walking around the corner.

It was a bizarre sight. In an effort he said later to disguise himself, he had dyed his hair. but instead of going blonde, it had gone sort of orange, so you had this man with dark skin, an Arab-looking man with orange hair. He just stood out like a sore thumb more than anything else.

That very morning when I talked to my team for the very first time, I said to them that I wasn't necessarily sure that I was any good at being a senior investigating officer, but I did seem to be lucky in the past. And I think I demonstrated that to them straight away on the first day because we went to talk to this man and there was Al Haddad. It was quite remarkable.

My officers spoke to Al Haddad and he was pretty open right from the start. He was never going to go "no comment" or tell lies or try and worm his way out of it. He was quite open and said: "Yeah, we killed her and it was all my girlfriend's idea." He then added: "My girlfriend and I fled to a house of a friend of hers in Surrey, in a place called Englefield Green."

He was promptly put into one of our cars and, rather than go home, there was a convoy through the snow out into Surrey to Englefield Green. We went to this modern estate and there was a small terraced house there, where Nympha Ong had a friend who spent a lot of time working abroad. He let her house-sit while he was away. She thought that was the ideal place to flee to after they had killed Bridie. They were both then arrested at the Englefield Green address, separated, and taken back to different police stations.

Right from the start, both of them did something that is quite common in two-handed murders. Each said it was the other's idea, the other's responsibility. No, they hadn't done anything themselves, but they'll tell you all about what their other half did.

When we started speaking to both of them, Al Haddad was reasonably open and was telling us roughly what had happened. But he was saying all the while that it was Nympha Ong, his older, more experienced, more cunning girlfriend who had duped him into following along with her plans. She was saying very little, she was no commenting and being non-committal about anything that went on.

What we had to do was to take the bones of what Al Haddad had been telling us and see if we could find evidence that would corroborate the story he gave us. Because if that was the case and we could corroborate it then we could probably prove that Nympha Ong was the driving force behind this murder.

He told us that Ong had been working for an estate agent in the locality and the whole idea of the murder was not just that they were fed up that Bridie had told them they had to leave and they had nowhere to live. It was also that Ong was convinced that Bridie had the deeds to the flat inside the premises. And she thought if they could get their hands on them, they could use them to procure some sort of loan or some sort of financial advantage and disappear into the sunset together with lots of money. That gave us their motive.

He told us some facts about how it had happened. He said that on Boxing Day they had kind of jumped onto Bridie while she was in the house. They'd asked her for the deeds for the house, she told them to go away and to get out. And then Al Haddad had taken her walking stick and beaten her with it. He had killed her.

Next, they had the pressing problem of disposing of Bridie's body. They went to see some friends who lived further up Edgware Road near Little Venice and asked if they could lend them a suitcase because they were going abroad. They borrowed a large suitcase and took it back to the flat where they put Bridie's body inside it.

Ong phoned for a minicab, specifying they needed an estate car because they had a lot of luggage. They were going to move the body in the suitcase somewhere, although Al Haddad said he didn't know where the intended destination was. To try and throw people off the scent, instead of ordering the minicab to come to Lanchester Court, she asked for it to come to Connaught Square, round the corner, the idea being they would take the suitcase around there and wait for the car. But there was a problem.

In the communal hall from Bridie's flat there was a flight of steps that went upwards to the front door and then you had to go down to the street. Bridie wasn't a large woman, she was quite small, nevertheless a dead weight in a suitcase was difficult for the murderers to manage. As they got it up this flight of carpeted steps, Nympha Ong realised there was blood leaking from the corner of the suitcase. They had to stop and reassess plans because they realised they couldn't take a suitcase leaking blood into a minicab and try to escape with it.

They returned with the suitcase to the flat. Ong said she thought the shed outside might be a good place to hide her. Al Haddad went to have a look and spotted the box. So they took the suitcase with Bridie in it around the back and transferred her into the TV box that we found her in.

They did their best to clean up the steps with the carpet on, cleaned up Bridie's flat and indeed cleaned up the suitcase they'd got from their friends before returning it to them. And then they disappeared to Englefield Green and that was that.

We spoke to those friends to see if they could substantiate the story. Not only did they corroborate it, but they told us that Al Haddad and Ong had come on Boxing Day, had a little bit of a party and as people do with their friends at Christmas, they'd been taking photographs. They gave us a roll of film, which we had developed. It was ominous because one of the shots showed Al Haddad and Ong with this large suitcase, a suitcase in which they tried to get rid of Bridie's body and in which we later found minute traces of Bridie's blood.

We asked for forensic work on the suitcase and, despite the clean-up job the couple had tried to do, in one of the seams that was difficult to get to, scientists found human blood. They tested it for a DNA profile, it was provably, definitely Bridie Skehan's blood in that suitcase.

We had a really good chain of evidence for this, we had the suitcase, it's got Bridies blood in it and in between times we know that Ong and Al Haddad had it because we have got photographic evidence of them standing there with the suitcase. Everything that we were being told was standing up and being corroborated.

Ironically, they never found the deeds to the house. They couldn't find them, but when we searched the house behind the sofa in the living room, where Bridie slept, there was more than £40,000 in cash. The two murderers missed it, thankfully, or they would have escaped with some gain.

Ahmed Al Haddad and Nympha Ong stood trial for the murder of Bridie Skehan at the Inner London Crown Court. The trial lasted for a couple of weeks and throughout it they blamed each other. It's what lawyers and police call a cut-throat defence where you have two defendants and they both point the finger at each other. Each said that it was the other one's idea to kill Bridie and that they could make some money out of it.

Obviously they were giving vastly different accounts, but there was an interesting diversion between the two of them. Ong said it was all Al Haddad's idea. She was too small and weak and too insignificant to have helped him, he killed Bridie and it was all his idea to use the suitcase and TV box.

He said virtually the opposite: "It was all her idea, she told me we can make some money out of this, we could get away together, she's 20 years older than me much more experienced, worldly-wise and she held that power over me. Yes, I had to do things and I hit Bridie with the walking stick because she told me to do it, she was too weak and small and she wouldn't have been able to do it, she needed my physical strength to do it."

There was also the question of how old Ong was. She was probably approaching 50 at the time but claimed she was in her 30s and no-one knew how old she really was. It all just threw another layer of intrigue on the case because you have this couple who are mismatched in many ways and their relationship led to this murder.

But the evidence was pretty clear really, the only question a jury had to decide was "who was responsible?"

Did they want to convict one or both of them or just one and if so which one?

It was the quickest deliberation of any jury for a murder trial I've ever been on. The jury made their decision in little more than half an hour – 38 minutes to be precise. They came back and convicted the pair of them; both were guilty of murder. In sentencing them, the judge remarked that this was a brutal murder of a vulnerable victim for some sort of financial gain. His recommendations reflected the parts that each had played in the murder.

Ong received a recommendation to serve for at least 17 years whereas for Al Haddad who was very much led on by her, the recommendation was only 10 years.

The judge obviously thought that she was the mastermind, the motivating force behind this murder and I have to say after having spoken to both of them and having seen their demeanour and knowing what I do about the case I absolutely agree with him.

This was a young man in his early 20s who was besotted by this woman twice his age and he was putty in her hands, he'd have done whatever she asked him to.

Bridie Skehan was just a lady who didn't deserve to end her long life in that way. She was a churchgoer, she looked after her lodgers, if you talked to them she was always fussing around them, she was active for her age.

She had let Nympha Ong into her home as a lodger, to provide her somewhere to live and because Ong and Al Haddad wouldn't live their lives under her roof in the way that she wanted, she'd asked them to leave. There wasn't any dramatic arguing about it; she just said: "Look that's not what I like going on under my roof, so we are going to have to have you go."

And as a result of that, Ong formed this murderous plan, this idea to threaten and offer violence to this old lady to get some documents that to be honest she couldn't have done much with anyway. It was a plan that was always going to fail in terms of providing a financial gain for her and Al Haddad. Yet Bridie lost her life for it – in her own home, battered to death with her own walking stick. And then she suffered the indignity of being chucked in a cardboard box to rot.

We were lucky because there were circumstances that got us over sort of humps and problems in the evidence of the case that meant we could prove it. I guess that was the kind of thing I meant when I said to the team that I don't know if I'm any good at being an SIO, but I'm certainly very lucky at it. When we saw that key hook with no key on it, that wasn't anything to do with luck, that was to do with solving the case, finding her body and from that point onwards, it was literally shaking the case like a rag doll to bring about the conclusion of justice.

It was one of these cases where you certainly felt a lot of antipathy towards the murderers; it was a completely unnecessary, over-the-top violent offence against a really innocent old and vulnerable victim. From a personal point of view it was really just what I needed at the very start of my career – a case with a degree of difficulty, where we overcame that difficulty and found the evidence. We had a conviction and it gave me an opportunity to see most of my members in my team in action for real instead of reading their appraisals or talking to my supervisors about who can do what. I saw it first-hand I spent virtually every minute of the investigation watching it go through.

And my first reaction was "they are actually quite good this lot and I hope I can continue to get the best from them and be good for them as well". I think the grounding with this case stood me in good stead going forward because we were certainly going to have more challenges and challenging cases together as time progressed, but I had the confidence of a team that could meet them and cope with them.

This idea of me being a lucky SIO I guess cropped up a number of times in this case, like we picked a random man walking along in Marylebone and it happened to be our suspect's brother, the fact that we had a photo of our suspects with the suitcase where the blood was found, things like that…

There's actually a phrase you hear quite often in the police: "You make your own luck." I don't subscribe to that view but I think you need to recognise luck when you have it and do the right thing with the good fortune you've been given. We had some lucky breaks, we did exactly the right thing and we ended up with a success and I finished the case of the murder of Bridie Skehan feeling very much that my time going forward with my new team would be worthwhile and they were a good bunch that I was looking forward to working with them.

Looking back, 21 years on from that moment, I wonder if that luck didn't kind of grow and work in a slightly different way and as well as being quite lucky in terms of being able to find bits of evidence and make cases, the sort of case, the number of cases and the sort of high profile cases that fell into my lap somehow, gave me the opportunity to do some work that even most people in the world of senior investigating officers don't get the chance to do. And to look at very high profile, public, important cases and important cases where arresting the suspect actually meant that you saved other people from becoming his victim. I see that now as the most important work you can do.

CHAPTER 6

THE MURDERS OF DAVID SHEEHAN & MICHAEL ZUBROT

In 2003, we moved to Fetcham, Surrey, which is actually where my ex-wife lived with her new husband. It meant the kids were less than a mile away from us and we saw them quite a lot. They had keys to our house as well as their own. Eventually Joe, my son, came to live with us, but that was later.

When Joe didn't do nearly as well as expected in his mock GCSEs, he had a big bust up with his mum and came and lived with us while he did his these and his A-levels. He went to uni in the end and it was all OK. He's now the loveliest, most caring, brilliant father and a well-respected police sergeant and everything that goes with it. But between the ages of about 13 and 18 years old, he was occasionally a bit of a nightmare. He understands that much more now he's a dad himself.

We tried to make time for the kids when I could. They'd come away with us and it was easier because we lived so close to them. The good thing was there was never any formal arrangement – "Oh you have the kids on this day, don't you?" – that made it easier to do that to a certain extent. And to give Maxine credit, she never wanted to try and prevent me seeing them as much as I did. We got to the stage where we used to dog-sit for each other. We both had pets and when we went away, she looked after our dog and vice versa. It was very cordial.

It was unpredictable hours so it wasn't always easy to see them. In the TV Bellfield drama, Manhunt, it's actually true that I was late home to see Kat and she'd made me a birthday cake on my birthday. It's probably more indicative of the fact that I was just so bloody blinkered and task-focused that not only did I forget that Kat was coming round but forgot the reason she was too – it was my birthday. It didn't actually register that it was my birthday and I shouldn't be sitting in Twickenham trying to find a white van, but it was the day after we identified Levi Bellfield, so it was a bit busy. I was very, very task-driven all the time.

All I wanted to do by this stage was to solve murders. I didn't have any time for all the extraneous shit that the bosses tried to get me involved with. I remember someone saying to me that I hadn't been to the last four health and safety committee meetings.

"Well, I've sent someone."

"But you should come yourself."

I replied: "If you can explain to me how that helps solve murders, I'll start coming."

That was actually after the Bellfield trial. That success had brought me a degree of untouchability. But he was the boss who eventually got rid of me and sent me over to Operation Minstead. I was just very focused on what we were doing. And I would do all the HR-y stuff, development of people and all that.

What I was actually there for was turning out and solving murders. And the reason I loved doing the job so much and didn't want to do anything else was that I knew that it was, to my mind, the only remaining job where I could hold that rank, have that degree of seniority and pay and still think I was a policeman. Who knows, if I'd been less passionate about being an SIO, I could have risen further.

Was I bright enough to do it? Possibly. Was I committed enough to do it? Probably not.

I'd decided about two years into my career that I wanted to solve murders, but because of the career path that I was on, I never thought it would happen until I got the phone call saying: "You can't be promoted, do you want to do something else?"

I never thought I'd be there. And God knows what would have happened if I'd not had that phone call and that hadn't happened. Because I always wanted to do that, but I didn't really know how I was going to achieve it. When I finally got to solve murders and serious crimes, it was everything I thought it would be.

I started and grew up in a force that was very much one where the team, the organisation, the job, was everything and you were just a part of that. Despite the fact that in attitude I was perhaps more modern than some of my colleagues, I actually much prefer that kind of culture or ethos among police officers than the one that puts themselves and their own progression in their own career first.

I think that's where the big change during my time in the police came. You were getting to the stage where there's this paralysis of decision-making where people don't want to do it. They're so frightened of getting that decision wrong and that being a black mark against them for their career progression that it's easier just not to make one.

When I started you had leaders who would lead. When I was at Holloway, we'd have a commander come down to Arsenal when there were big, category A games, Tottenham at home, West Ham at home, Man United. He'd say that the Metropolitan Police was into participative management now, but that's got no place in a public order situation. He said – and I remember this: "The wrong decision is better than no decision." In other words, make sure people know what they're doing, make a decision. If it goes wrong, it's gone wrong. But if you stand there and don't know what you're doing, then it certainly will go wrong.

I always lived by that, and far too many leaders in policing are prepared to make no decision in case they make the wrong decision. I think that's where we've lost a lot.

Some people have called me a maverick. I'm not sure maverick's the right word but I'm actually quite simple. My role as an SIO in the Met was to make my team the most effective and efficient machine for solving murders. Period. That was my job. Anything else beyond that was just extraneous and didn't really interest me. I just wanted to do that.

I did a lot of arguing behind closed doors that perhaps the people that were on my team didn't know about, but that's exactly how I wanted it. The phrase I used was a buffer between my team and the management essentially. They didn't need to know what had happened because how was that going to help them work more efficiently? I'm not sure it would have done. All they needed to know was that this was the outcome. And if it was an outcome we didn't like I'd tell them I'd fought for them and I'd tried my best. A lot of the time when the outcome was what they wanted, I didn’t tell them what had happened, I didn't need to. All I needed to do was to make sure they had the best conditions possible to do their job. That's what I tried to do.

The David Sheehan murder in January 2003 was the second new investigation I was given after I’d assumed charge of the team at Barnes and, like all of the investigations, some detectives on the team play very pivotal roles and some do the other roles. Two very experienced detectives that came to the fore in this one were DC Simon Rogers and DC Gary Cunningham.

They took on the key roles of dealing with the forensic exhibits and Gary Cunningham would also interview the suspects, he was one of the trained interviewers on the team and he was particularly good at doing that. The call came to us – we were in the frame as they call it, as we had the capacity to take a new investigation, having just finished the Bridie Skehan case.

Police had been called to an old house that had been converted into flats on Boston Road in Hanwell, west London. They were housing association flats that were reserved for people who had issues and difficulties in their lives. We were told there were two men that lived there who were known to the police because they were both heavy drinkers. They'd get drunk and fall out with each other. They'd had some quite violent disputes in the past and police had been called, so it was perhaps no real shock that one of these violent fights had ended in tragedy.

On this particular evening, there'd been a very violent falling out between the two men and one of them was dead. He'd been stabbed numerous times; around the chest and neck, in what appeared to be his own bed in the flat. David Sheehan was a 35-year-old man, who through his life had issues with alcohol abuse and mental health. He'd been allocated this bedsit in the property, housing people with similar issues. One of these people was Mohammed Khaleel. You do question whether it was the right place for somebody like that to be, because these two volatile, heavy drinkers, in close proximity to each other seemed to be a recipe for tragedy or disaster. And that was what happened that fateful night..

Police entered the first-floor flat after the call and found a scene of absolute horror. Sheehan was on his own bed and had been stabbed more than 40 times about the chest, neck and abdomen. The weapon which was nearby was a chef's steel used for sharpening knives, it was in itself quite a blunt instrument. Mohammed Khaleel, who also lived in a first-floor flat, was a very interesting but also a quite disturbing character. He had a strong interest in the occult and in black magic and was reading up on that. He seemed to be obsessed with it. Oddly, as well as reading up on black magic and the occult, he was also a great fan of the music of Elvis Presley. He'd spend his leisure time going to see various Elvis impersonators in various pubs and clubs in the area.

Both David Sheehan and Khaleel had befriended a local Baptist minister and had attended church services on a Sunday together there. I don't think there was any great religious conviction, particularly on Khaleel's part, but it was just somebody who was trying to help them and help them make their way through life and to deal with the situations they'd had. It might have given them some comfort, but Khaleel had become quite fervent about the occult. He'd been taking books on the subject out of the library and reading them and seemed to have a fantasy of becoming a horror writer. The minister had noticed this and he too was troubled by how Khaleel's mind might have been working at that point and was concerned over this apparently unhealthy interest.

On the night of January 29 2003, Mohammed Khaleel had left the flat and gone to Ealing to buy some cider to drink. He was seen on the CCTV coming back to the flat in Boston Road at about 11.20pm with a blue carrier bag with the cider in it. He went into the flat and that seems to be when the argument broke out between him and Sheehan for some reason.

Sheehan was on his bed in his bedsit and Khaleel had stabbed him. There were as many as perhaps 47 separate stab wounds from the chef's steel and then he'd finished the job off with a 10-inch kitchen knife and slashed Sheehan across the throat.

The most striking thing about this murder was the amount of injuries, the level of savagery in the frenzied attack was really startling. There were 40-odd stab wounds inflicted with a blunt piece of metal, and such was the force needed to make those stab wounds that we later found a hand print, one of Khaleel's handprints, on the ceiling. So, David Sheehan had been lying on his bed, Khaleel was standing on it and to get more power, more force to make these stab wounds go in, he'd been pushing himself against the ceiling to get extra purchase. It really highlighted not just the barbaric nature of the attack, but how determined it was. I'd never seen anything like it before and never have since.

After this horrible, violent attack took place, Khaleel ran out into the street shouting: "David is dead!". It was actually him, Khaleel, who raised the alarm. He stopped a passer-by and said: "Can you call an ambulance, my friend up there is dead." Yet only minutes before he'd been plunging this thing into his chest and cutting his throat. After the alarm was raised and paramedics and police attended, of course, Khaleel had disappeared, he had fled the scene and was nowhere to be found.

When we took the investigation over the following morning, there was still no sign of Khaleel back at the house or flat where he lived. We knew who he was, however it was difficult in the sense that he didn't have a job, he didn't have any regular places where we knew we could look for him. We spoke to neighbours who told us about the volatility in the relationship between these two men in the past and we spoke to the Baptist minister who confirmed that.

My intelligence team did the normal sort of trawl and checks they would perform, and we discovered that Khaleel was due to visit his probation officer for a formal check-in meeting a couple of days later. This made a plan relatively simple for us – we could go along to the probation office, it was a meeting he had to attend by law and he'd be in trouble if he didn't. There was a strong possibility that even if he knew what he'd done back home with David Sheehan, he was still going to turn up for this meeting. Officers went down there, waited for him to come and when he did turn up, as we hoped he would, they arrested him.

We knew the identity of the prime suspect and there was very little doubt from the very beginning that Khaleel was going to be the man who committed the murder. But of course, knowing who did it is sometimes a very different thing from proving who did it. Although we had the name and we were able to find where he was and arrest him within a couple of days, the scientific work that was going on back at the flat was going to be crucial.

We had ample forensic evidence to link Khaleel to the scene but this wouldn't be conclusive as prior to the assault, Khaleel would have had a lawful reason to be in Sheehan's flat. They were friends and so he would be expected to have been handling things in there, leaving his DNA and fingerprints. There was nothing to be gained by evidencing Khaleel's presence in the room, we had to prove he had been in the room at the time Sheehan was being attacked.

Khaleel's handprint in Sheehan's blood was instrumental in that, it was a crucial piece of forensic evidence; there could be very few, if any, other explanations as to how that could have got there aside from during this violent and murderous attack.

Khaleel's side of the story was that he had been subjected over a period of weeks and months to a number of violent attacks and assaults by David Sheehan. When he returned there with the cider that evening, he sensed as they talked to each other that another row was brewing. He thought he was going to get assaulted by Sheehan again and pre-emptively he struck out in self-defence.

The law does allow somebody to use force to defend themselves, even pre-emptively, if they have a reasonable fear that they are going to be attacked. My difficulty with this case was that Khaleel had stabbed him 47 times and then cut his throat. For me it was difficult really to say that was reasonable force and that it was reasonably done to prevent him being attacked. But that was his story and that's what he stuck to.

Mohammed Khaleel appeared in 2004 at Southwark Crown Court.

The court had heard how he and David Sheehan had become good friends after moving into the same house in Boston Road in Hanwell, but both were such heavy drinkers, they would often get into fights with each other, sometimes armed with knives and even a claw hammer on one occasion.

Khaleel was cleared of murder, but the aspiring horror writer was found guilty of manslaughter due to provocation. Passing sentence, Judge George Bathurst Norman said: "This was, in my view, one of the most savage attacks I have ever seen in the courts in 40 years at the bar."

As a result of being found guilty of manslaughter rather than murder, Khaleel didn't have a mandatory life sentence. He was sentenced to just eight years' imprisonment. Even though the judge said that it was the most savage attack he'd encountered during 40 years at the bar, the plea of manslaughter on the grounds of provocation succeeded and, I have to say, we were pretty shocked by this. We all came across cases of manslaughter doing this job and this seemed to be an attack with an intent far beyond what was necessary to deal with the immediate threat and beyond something that might be termed as provocation.

It was particularly ironic and hard for David Sheehan's family to understand because some years previously, his brother had been convicted of murder – a murder for which his brother was serving life imprisonment – which took place as the result of a fight in a pub, where Sheehan's sibling punched a man once who fell over and died. It's known as a one-punch manslaughter, the sort of thing that courts would regularly view as manslaughter rather than murder because simply punching someone once often doesn't show an intent to cause really serious harm or to kill – and therefore it can't be murder.

These cases seemed to Sheehan's family – and indeed to us - to be the wrong way around. You would think of the two, his brother – the one punch – would be the manslaughter and the stabbing somebody 47 times with a chef's steel and then cutting their throat looks more like murder.

Mohammed Khaleel served his eight-year term of imprisonment. When he was released, it was almost as if he was just spending those eight years marking time, ready to go back to his old ways.

Initially, his freedom lasted only for six weeks because he was again arrested for a minor offence and that was enough to trigger his recall to prison. He served another 18 months or so and then was released in 2010.

When Mohammed Khaleel was finally freed he was given a room in a hostel in Ealing. It was in a lovely street, full of expensive houses, with a doctor's surgery nearby and a cricket club next door – the most genteel of surroundings.

But it was a place in which he was able to sit and plot his twisted, occult-driven plan to find another victim to murder.

Within four months or so, Mohammed Khaleel got into the habit of going to Walpole Park in Ealing, where he would drink with some men who frequented the park. One of those was Michael Zubrot, whom he befriended. Zubrot was a 67-year-old man, he was gregarious, openly gay and he lived in Perivale, west London.

Zubrot and Khaleel became drinking partners. They shared an interest in drinking to excess and quite often they would go to Zubrot's flat and sit there drinking the night away. Khaleel would only ever say he was an associate, there was no suggestion from him that it was any more than that or any kind of relationship. Of course what Zubrot didn't know was that Khaleel was intent on finding another vulnerable man to victimise, to murder. In Michael Zubrot, this open, friendly and affable chap, he found the ideal target.

It was in Zubrot's flat in Perivale that something snapped again in Mohammed Khaleel's head and in

Zubrot's own home, he murdered him savagely, stabbing him many times.

History repeated itself, it was very much the same way that Khaleel had murdered David Sheehan, nine years earlier.

Michael Zubrot was lying down with his arms outstretched, palms uppermost. He'd been stabbed multiple times in his body and his throat had been cut, again echoing the sort of attack on David Sheehan that we had seen earlier. Responding to a call that Michael had not been seen for some days, police went to his flat and inside they found his decomposing body. At that time of year, early September, the weather is quite warm and this undoubtedly accelerated the decomposition.

Experts can make an assessment either through the rate of decomposition or any insect activity as to the likely date of death as opposed to the date it was found. From their conclusions the investigating team went backwards in time, looking at bus CCTV in the area, and finally they were able to find some footage of Michael Zubrot on August 30 2010. He was not alone on the bus; he was with Mohammed Khaleel. And they alighted from the bus at the stop closest to Michael Zubrot's flat.

It was only when Khaleel was then researched and arrested that it came to light for that team that we had arrested him for a murder seven years previously, one for which he'd been imprisoned for just six and a half years.

Mohammed Khaleel appeared at the Old Bailey towards the end of 2011 charged with Michael Zubrot's murder. His defence was that somebody else had done it but the evidence was overwhelming.

He was convicted, found guilty and sentenced to life imprisonment with a recommendation that he serve at least 33 years before considered for parole. Judge Peter Thornton said that Zubrot's killing was cold-blooded.

Michael Zubrot's friends and family feel like the system didn't really work for them. It's just hugely ironic with the contrast between what happened to Zubrot and what happened to David Sheehan's brother. I don't think I'm alone in feeling that Michael Zubrot and his family were badly let down by the system, because here you have a man who was clearly prone to extreme violence, he'd killed somebody, he was arrested, taken before the courts and through what I'm sure laypeople would see almost as a legal loophole, he managed to come up with a way to excuse his behaviour, meaning he served only six and a half years in prison. Within weeks of being released from that sentence, he'd killed somebody else in a very similar manner.

The really galling thing about it is that I don't think we could have done anything any differently. We reacted to a report of a murder, we established who the murderer was very quickly, we found him within a couple of days, we charged him within a couple of days. We found ample evidence, scientific evidence, at the scene linking him to it. We did everything that we could, put him before the court and the decision then which is out of our hands, is that he only serves six and a half years in prison.

Doing the job that we did, with these murders and these serious cases, you have to accept and understand that the system is such that we don't choose how long they go to prison for. Other people do that and they have their reasons. But when something like this happens, then I think those other people who make those decisions need to reflect on whether they might have erred. To me it is very, very simple. He'd stabbed a man 40-odd times and cut his throat. Is that really manslaughter, for which he deserves just eight years?

I had to speak with David Sheehan's mother and explain to her how that happened when her other son punched somebody once and is serving life for murder. And you can't explain that because it makes no sense. That was the case there and then in 2004. And when you then get to 2010 and he's been let out and killed somebody within six weeks, then I think you have the right to be completely aghast and staggered about it. Not only was this bizarre almost perverse decision made in 2004, the consequence of that is that some poor bloke who didn't deserve anything has lost his life as well.

That's the top and bottom of that case. The other notable fact was that this was a horrifically high level of violence, especially on the basis that the force needed to push a Sabatier chef's steel through somebody's skin 47 times is quite immense.

The system's shit sometimes.

CHAPTER 7

THE MURDER OF CATHERINE CORRIDAN

I started as the Senior Investigating Officer, the leader of the team at Barnes, south west London in January 2003. When I went there, the Kate Corridan disappearance was a cold case that had been resurrected about six months before.

It was something on the books already – it was one of the things I had to get my head around, to read into the cases that the team already had on their books.

Catherine Corridan was reported missing in 1994 after attending a party and an investigation, Operation Gateside, was launched into her disappearance. It ran for some time and not much progress was made with it – eventually it was decided that it wasn't going to go anywhere and it was put away.

In April 2002 an investigator called Graham Wilson came across the case papers and the exhibits in storage somewhere in west London.

The materials were examined and it was really there that the genesis of what became Operation New

Gateside, the reinvestigation, came about. It was just due to a diligent officer finding some papers and thinking: "This is interesting, can we do anything with it?"

Generally in these cases, it requires two things. It takes somebody – normally a relatively junior officer – to have the idea, to find the exhibits or the paperwork, or both. And then they will approach somebody in a more senior position and say: "Let's look at this, it really ought to be taken on, we ought to reopen this investigation."

Sometimes there are advances in science – a DNA profile can be obtained from old exhibits. In this case, it was simply somebody looking at the papers and saying: "This isn't finished, it hasn't come up to a full stop, this is an investigation that can be taken further." My predecessor agreed that it appeared to be something that should be looked into, so by the time I came in to lead the team, there had been nearly six months of work done to try and progress the investigation from when it had been put away almost ten years before.

When you have a heavy workload of new cases, relentlessly coming one after another, there is a temptation to say: "That one that's been going on for 10 or 20 years, we can push that to one side." But there is still justice to be found, there are still family members who want answers and there are still potentially murderers at large, so it was always something I wanted to try and keep us doing at the same time as the new cases that were coming in to us.

I think there's an argument for saying really at that point, you ought to make a judgement as to whether the new case is still more important than the old one you were looking at before. I guess it would be a fair criticism to say that I always wanted to do everything. So, the idea of putting an old cold case like Kate Corridan on the back burner while we dealt with the new ones was not something I found attractive. That brought me into a degree of conflict with those above me.

There was some pressure, of course the Corridan case was eating into the overtime budget and potentially the forensic budget, but I wanted to keep it going. We had a small team allocated to it who were working virtually exclusively on that case. They were very committed – I'd spoken to them and they'd convinced me that there was potential in it; that it was eminently solvable. So I resisted pressure to shut it down and let them carry on. As things transpired, I'm really glad they did because yes, they did solve it.

The whole way that the murder team worked was that you would have investigations running along in parallel, that was just the nature of the beast. It was very different to what you might see in drama or indeed in documentaries where everything is pretty much linear and it's just a team on one case. You would always have these sorts of cases going on where a handful would be active at the same time. My role was very much to be the coordinator of the teams that were concentrating on each of these separate investigations. So, Dave and Mark Leach became one of those sub-teams and they were concentrating on Catherine Corridan's disappearance.

The way in which we were able to keep the Corridan investigation going was to essentially write off the Leach Brothers from other cases and, as well as that, rely on their determination and passion to get the job done. The size of the team was such that I judged that I could afford to allow them pretty much free rein to carry on with the Corridan case and not call on them too often to come and help with the new cases. When a new investigation was opened it really was necessary to call upon them – there is just so much to do in those first couple of days, but they were the first ones that I would release so they could keep the Corridan case going.

I think it was obvious from talking to them – I didn't know them when I first went there – they were both experienced murder squad detectives and just chatting through what they had, what they found, what their lines of inquiry were, what they aimed to do, it became obvious to me that they were two very capable officers who I could trust absolutely with moving the investigation on.

Catherine Corridan was born in 1963 in the Irish Republic and was in her mid-20s – around 1986-87– when she came over to England. She came to live in a flat in north west London with her sister. The flat was owned by the Royal National Institute for the Blind and it was at their school nearby that Catherine found work as a cook – the flat came with the job. She also had a second job as a cook at a residential home for the elderly nearby. She was a hardworking girl, she came here to work and live her life and, like a lot of people when they emigrate, she gravitated towards people from her own community. There was no shortage of people from Ireland living in that part of London and it was in that community that she befriended the man who ultimately was going to kill her.

Catherine initially lived in the flat with her sister Bridget, but Bridget then met and married an American man and emigrated to the USA. It was at that point that Catherine was allocated the flat in her own right and she began to live there alone.

Catherine first met Martin Kerrigan in a bar in Cricklewood called Ashtons on St Patrick's Day in 1991. They very quickly became boyfriend and girlfriend; within a matter of days they were going out with each other. The relationship developed and she moved in with Martin Kerrigan and his parents who were also living in London.

Kerrigan's family was just about the complete opposite to the Corridan family. There were several brothers and sisters but they were dysfunctional, they were criminals and alcohol played a huge part the way they lived their lives.

It was through Martin Kerrigan that Catherine met his brother, Samuel. At that time – in 1992 – Samuel was serving a sentence in Wandsworth jail. Eventually in August 1992, Catherine decided she'd had enough of Martin and ended the relationship for good. He left the relationship and eventually returned to his wife in Ireland – he was already married – but as a parting gift he stole Catherine's cheque book and cheque card and went on a spending spree, working his way through £410 of her money. She wasn't a wealthy lady and that was a considerable sum to her.

Samuel Kerrigan was released from prison in March 1993. Less than five months later, in August, he was involved with another man in an armed robbery with firearms at a branch of the Midland Bank, stealing more than £3,000. They escaped in a getaway car driven by a woman who was never identified. What we do know is that the woman wasn't Catherine Corridan because she, at the time, was visiting her sister in the United States.

Martin Kerrigan returned to Ireland permanently and around that time Samuel Kerrigan and Catherine formed a relationship. Samuel himself described her as just his "partner-in-crime", that she would just collect him and drive him around various criminal enterprises. It wasn't a sexual relationship.

On the March 5th 1994, Samuel Kerrigan was with a friend named Martin Brazil, drinking in a pub called the White Hart. They went back to Brazil's house to carry on drinking through the afternoon. At some point, Brazil said: "Look, I've been invited to a house party tonight but we haven't got any money so I can't buy any booze to take with us." Kerrigan came up with the idea of ringing Catherine, showing the exploitative nature of their relationship. "She will have money, she can give us money to buy booze and we can all go to the party together."

When the three of them arrived at the party, there was a bit of an argument that started because Samuel Kerrigan didn't want to take the drink they'd bought into the party while Catherine thought they ought to. After they had gone into the party the argument flared up again. At some point, Catherine threw a drink over Kerrigan.

It quietened down again, they were at the party for some time and then at a point well into the next day, something like four in the morning, Catherine Corridan and Samuel Kerrigan disappeared in Martin Brazil's Vauxhall Cavalier. Brazil didn't know they had left and he was really angry that they'd effectively stolen his car with all the booze in it that never got taken into the party.

Later, Samuel Kerrigan rang Martin Brazil's girlfriend, Fiona Dolan, and told her that he was at Catherine's flat and that Catherine had gone off to go to America, giving Samuel her cheque book and card to look after. Fiona Dolan eventually went in a minicab to retrieve Martin Brazil's car. She found it near Ealing Hospital where it had run out of petrol. The thinking at the time – and even at the time of the trial – was that Kerrigan may have driven from the party back to Hallowell Road, then all the way back in towards Ealing again and that's when the car ran out of petrol.

But the fact is that we know there was only about £3 worth of petrol in the car at the start of the evening and that was a journey of such a length as probably wouldn't have been possible.

It seemed more likely that what happened was that Catherine and Samuel Kerrigan were in the Cavalier when it ran out of petrol near the hospital, they decided to walk and, to cut off effectively a big corner of their journey, they took a path between two golf courses. Kerrigan would have known that the footpath existed and to cut the corner off because it came out on the main road exactly by the council depot which was his place of work.

The rest of that day Fiona Dolan, Samuel Kerrigan and Martin Brazil, went on a spending spree around the West End, with Catherine Corridan's cheque book and card. They actually spent more on food and alcohol than on anything else.

At the end of the day, Samuel Kerrigan produced a ring and a gold neck chain and gave them to Fiona Dolan as a thank you present for driving him around all day and being understanding about it. That gift is something that became really important to the reinvestigation team years later.

Catherine Corridan's disappearance was first noticed by her employers at the school when she didn't turn up for work. The headmaster got the caretaker from the school to go round to the flat and try to effect entry to see if all was well. He went in and found that there were some signs of disturbance – a vase had been broken and put into the bin – but beyond that, nothing of note. He called police and they went through quite a lot of scientific, forensic work. They found some blood-stained socks but couldn't discover whose blood it was.

Police eventually arrested Samuel Kerrigan after they had received information from the bank that Catherine Corridan's cheque book and card had been used extensively. He managed to explain it away by saying: "Well, yes she's gone to America and she said I could have the money left over in her account". Otherwise he gave "no comment" answers to any question put to him. His house was searched and there was nothing of any use found there and eventually, the investigating officers came to the conclusion that there were no more lines of inquiry that were going to lead them to solve the case and the investigation was shelved.

On May 12 1994, Samuel Kerrigan returned to Uxbridge Police Station – he'd been on police bail while enquiries were conducted. He again refused to answer any questions, before being told: "You're free to go now, the bail is over." This ended the Operation Gateside investigation.

More than two years later, in July 1996, a Metropolitan Police Flying Squad detective investigating armed robberies and looking at CCTV footage from reported crimes identified Samuel Kerrigan as one of the men on the Midland Bank robbery back in 1993.

Kerrigan was arrested and, 18 months later, convicted of armed robbery. It wasn't simply for robbing the bank, but also an elderly lady who was a customer there. Not content with the cash handed to him by staff behind the counter, he stole money from the terrified customer's handbag as well. He was sentenced to 12 years' imprisonment, although that sentence was reduced on appeal to nine years, meaning he was due to be released from prison in early 2004.

As Operation New Gateside kicked off, amongst all the exhibits and case papers found languishing at an old police station was a roll of undeveloped film from a camera. It had been seized by officers on the original Gateside investigation because they believed it to contain photographs taken during the party where Catherine Corridan was last seen alive.

The party was at a house occupied by a group of ex-pats from Australia and New Zealand, making it difficult for officers. They ended up having to take the photographs halfway around the world to speak to witnesses who had returned home and try to establish and work out who exactly was depicted. This old roll of film opened up huge and complicated lines of inquiry - but lines that really brought us closer to finding out what had happened.

In July 2002, Bridget, Catherine Corridan's sister, identified the other man at the armed robbery at the Midland bank as Martin Kerrigan. He was now back in Ireland, so officers went there to interview him about the armed robbery. He denied it and gave a DNA sample for testing. This would in turn lead to attempts by police to extradite Martin from Ireland so he could be charged and answer to the allegation that he took part in the armed robbery. Those attempts came to nothing but they form another important part of the wider story of Catherine Corridan's disappearance.

At the beginning of 2003 – literally a couple of weeks after I'd come onto the team and was trying to familiarise myself with this case – the officers investigating Catherine's disappearance got a statement from an important witness, a neighbour of Samuel Kerrigan, Martin Wright, who stated he had been told by Kerrigan that "he bashed the fuck out of that girl".

Samuel Kerrigan was already on the list of persons of interest but the information from his neighbour about his boast dragged him up to the top. He suddenly became our prime suspect for having killed Catherine Corridan.

We then asked the prison service if they would move Samuel Kerrigan. He was serving his sentence in a rural prison outside of London and we wanted him back closer so it was easier for us to monitor his visits and phone calls. We wanted to increase surveillance on him to see if he would give anything else away about what he'd done to Catherine.

The team were busy too with Martin Kerrigan, and in November 2003 Uxbridge Magistrates Court issued a warrant for his arrest for the Midland Bank robbery. In January 2004, he was arrested in Ireland on three counts of robbery relating to the Midland Bank job that Samuel was convicted and serving a sentence for.

In March 2004, Samuel Kerrigan was produced from prison, taken to Ealing Police Station and questioned about the murder of Catherine Corridan. He made no comment. He now knew two things. He was due to come out of prison in a matter of days and was now facing being charged with another serious offence. And secondly, he knew that his brother, who was with him on the bank job, was now going to be prosecuted for that as well.

As intended, this concentrated his mind and put a great deal of pressure on him, so much so that when Dave and Mark Leach went in the next day to speak to him about the murder, he had all of this whirling around in his mind. It was police officers doing their job completely lawfully, completely within the law, but using the circumstances to their best advantage to try and get justice and try and get the right people convicted.

What nobody really expected during that day was that Samuel Kerrigan was going to drop the bombshell he did. He sat and told the officers: "If we can do some sort of deal around my brother, I can tell you where the body is buried."

The whole premise of this case had been that it would be a no body prosecution because we had no idea where to find Catherine's remains. For him to drop that on us was remarkable, I vividly remember receiving the phone call: "You'll never guess what he just told us." He gave us a story, saying he wasn't responsible for the death, he was only responsible for burying the body.

Nevertheless, if we are able to find the body, not only does that give some sense of peace for the family, but also there might be forensic opportunities to tie either Samuel Kerrigan – if it was him – or somebody else into the murder.

We knew it probably wasn't going to be easy because he'd given us a rough location – a site next to West Middlesex Golf Club and Hanwell Cricket Club. It was in a semi-rural area despite being in London and ad hoc burials like this are always difficult to find and place. But it meant that we had an opportunity to find the body that we'd previously thought impossible. So it was a no-brainer really, we had to go over there and see if we could find it, even if it would undoubtedly be a large and costly operation to find a crudely buried body in a field.

The search for Catherine's body went on for some weeks and it was an operation with a significant hunger for resources. The location Kerrigan had pointed out was in a piece of wasteland between two golf courses, there was a cricket club nearby. He had oriented himself by looking at some tower blocks and did the same when he went with his solicitor and officers. He turned around and looked at the nearby tower blocks saying: "Yeah, I could see that one there, so it must be here somewhere."

He'd given us the right area, but the undergrowth and bracken around had regrown and made it difficult. We had to have big diggers in there, we had forensic archaeologists, botanists and police search experts. It was fortunate for us that the cricket club was there because they were glad to open the pavilion for us to use as our base. I went down on a number of occasions and we were using cadaver dogs on the area. We really did the very best we could to find her. We very nearly got to the point of giving up because we'd gone down a foot or so over a wide area and still not found her.

At this point the archaeologist said: "Let's just try some more." It was the stickiest point in all of this for us because this operation was so expensive and so resource intensive, the equipment we were renting, the expertise we were hiring in, the officers that we had on standby and the uniformed search officers that were there every day. I was getting it in the neck. I always said that part of my job was to be the buffer, to stop that affecting my team, who are doing their job and doing their best. I do the politics and I do the arguing and let them get on and do what they do best – solving murders. There was a lot of pressure on me to call it a day. But while the experts were saying it was still worth going, that there might still be something there, I wasn't going to let them stop.

The forensic archaeologist said: "I think we should go down a little bit deeper, let's go down another two inches."

It's a good thing he did, because those two inches were key to it. We took two inches off with a digger and almost immediately found Catherine's remains.

Catherine Corridan's body was discovered in this shallow grave and underneath where her neck had been we noticed a glint. It was a tiny piece of gold and when we examined it, it was the clasp from a necklace. Not only had he raided Catherine's bank account with her cheques, but he'd also stolen the jewellery from her body, and given it all to Fiona Dolan the next day. It showed us how callous this man was, but it was also fantastic evidence, We had a statement from Fiona Dolan saying the necklace was given to her by Samuel Kerrigan with the clasp missing, and we had an expert saying the rest of it was underneath Catherine Corridan's body in a makeshift grave.

Our best guess as to what happened that night was that Catherine and Samuel Kerrigan had had an argument at the party We knew that became finger-wagging and drink-throwing but that it had not really been violent. We thought the pair left together in Martin Brazil's Cavalier. We knew that it broke down near Ealing Hospital, we also knew that it only had £3 worth of petrol in it at the start of the night, so the likelihood was that it probably didn't drive up to Northwood and back. It was much more likely that it ran out of petrol after they left the party at Hanwell. That put Catherine Corridan and Samuel Kerrigan together on foot right at a point by the start of the footpath from the main road outside Ealing Hospital, through the golf courses, round to the depot where Kerrigan worked. Crucially this route took them exactly past the spot where Catherine's body had been found.

We couldn't be certain what happened during that journey. But we did know the arrangement of Catherine's clothing when her remains were found showed that she had one boot on and one boot off, one leg out of her jeans. It certainly looked to the world like somebody who has been raped, it was the classic arrangement of clothing where there has been a struggle and a rape taken place. Did the argument continue? How did the rape happen? Was it planned or did it just happen while they were just walking and arguing? Did Kerrigan just think to himself: "Well, I've gone too far now, I've raped her and she's going to tell the police and I'm going to be in serious trouble, I need to silence her." And was that why he killed her?

The argument they had was really trivial and doesn't seem to justify her being murdered. Nothing could justify that, but there's a huge escalation from a tiff about bringing drink into a party and a drink being thrown to murdering and burying someone on a golf course. What happened in between these events?

Samuel Kerrigan was charged with Catherine Corridan's murder and his trial began on January 10 2005 at Blackfriars Crown Court.

He never admitted what happened on that night; he never showed any remorse for her. There was a bit of regret, but it was a selfish, self-pitying regret: "I've had to carry the fact that I buried this young woman around with me for all these years." It wasn't about her or her family, it was all about him.

He was found guilty of Catherine Corridan's murder and was sentenced to life imprisonment. I was asked for a comment and I said that to recover Catherine Corridan's body was, for her family, especially important. But also to convict Samuel Kerrigan who'd got away with it for so long, was a really satisfying success and that both were due almost entirely to the determined and diligent efforts of just a handful of detectives who resurrected this case and then, when they had their suspect in custody, skilfully interviewed him so that he gave up the location of Catherine's body.

This case is a really good example of why closed cases, old cases, cold cases, call them whatever you will, should be given importance and resources by the police.

It's very often the case that if you have the right people and the right motivation, they can be solved. There are families who still want justice, and in too many cases, who still want to know where their loved ones are buried. It's possible for officers to satisfy them and to give them that peace. It can be done in and among all the new cases coming in, it is possible still to keep an investigation going alongside the new current cases that have to be looked at.

I think in this case, we were fortunate that we had really committed and really talented detectives. I was able to allow them the space, despite all the other new work that was coming in, I was still able to let them carry on with this. We had the Levi Bellfield investigation before this investigation was resolved, the temptation to pull these officers on to that was huge, but if we had done, we wouldn't have had this resolution for the Corridan family.

To me the big lesson out of Catherine's case was that it's OK sometimes to give your staff a bit of rope, because a lot of people, including my then boss, thought that was a waste of resources. I did at first, I wasn't sure until I sat down and spoke to the team and they explained what they were doing. I said: "You crack on with it because it was a case that could be solved; it needed to be solved." I learnt from that.

It would have been very easy to say that I need all my resources in the current cases and the new ones. I'm so glad I did and they did a fantastic job. They were really committed to it and I think sensing that commitment and sensing that desire in them was probably something that swayed me to think "well okay, let them have another go for a little more".

Another interesting thing is the decision to let the forensic team carry on. We could just as easily have left it there. It was just that couple of inches, I've always said that it's better to be lucky than smart.

Dave Leach and other officers on the case were invited by the Corridan family to attend Catherine's funeral in Caherdaniel in County Kerry, Ireland. Her final resting place in the family plot is at Derrynane Abbey, a burial ground that is cut off by the sea at high tide and a site of outstanding natural beauty. When the priest mentioned that the Metropolitan Police officers who had solved the case after all these years and enabled Catherine's body's repatriation, her family and other mourners all clapped and tapped their bibles. The job doesn't get any better than that, really.

CHAPTER 8
THE MURDER OF CLARE BERNAL

By 2004, Levi Bellfield had been arrested and we were tirelessly assembling the evidence in that case, but we were still working other investigations alongside it.

The only concession we got for taking on a serial murder case was one rota out of the on-call. We had been on-call the week before we took on what became the Bellfield case, nine weeks later we should have been on call again and they got someone else to cover us, so we didn't have to do it. And that was it. That was the only slack anyone would cut us.

For the first six weeks of the Bellfield case, we had a lot more staff, virtually twice the usual number of people. And then by the time we were due on call again, 18 weeks, nearly five months later, we were back in the on-call system again. And the chances are that during that period you would have to take on another investigation or three.

It was a Tuesday evening in September 2005, and I was on-call SIO for west London and I remember getting the call and Control, which gave out the jobs said: “I’ve got a double fatal shooting for you Mr Sutton.” At the time we had been suffering from a few shootings in west London, most of them in Harlesden and areas like that. I assumed that’s where I’d be going, and so I asked: “Whereabouts in Harlesden am I going?”

“No, it’s a bit of a funny one. It’s at Harvey Nichols.”

Most of the team had gone home by then, it was in the evening, but I had a system whereby we’d ring around and I scrambled the team to come to Harvey Nichols.

Harvey Nichols is in London’s Knightsbridge. It is a world-famous department store with a wealthy clientele in a very wealthy area of the capital. How can that happen? Why would there have been a double fatal shooting at Harvey Nichols?

Clare Bernal came from a middle-class family background, she was a bright, intelligent, articulate, very attractive young lady who wanted to work in the field of make-up and cosmetics. She had been working at Harvey Nichols for some time and absolutely loved the job. Clare was a little inexperienced in the ways of the world and certainly in relationships with men. She’d had a relationship at the start of the year with a man who worked as a security guard at the store, he’d become very obsessive and serious about their relationship very quickly.

Michael Pech was 10 years or so older than Clare. He’d seen a lot of life, including a spell in the military. He obviously just fell completely in love with her, he was absolutely besotted with her. She didn't want the relationship to be that serious that quickly – she didn't know what she wanted, but I think she knew that she didn't want to be tied to Michael Pech in the way that he did to her. But you can't always predict how somebody is going to react to those sorts of circumstances.

On the fateful day, Michael Pech went into the store it was his job to guard, shot dead his ex-girlfriend Clare Bernal and then turned the gun on himself.

It looked like a classic murder-suicide but you mustn't make any assumptions in cases like this; they still need to be investigated. It was obviously a really tragic case, but it was also one of those where it would be even more foolish than usual to jump to conclusions. Although it looks for the world that there has been a murder followed by a suicide, you still have to respond to it, to investigate the most serious of offences even if it seems obvious the perpetrator is dead. You need to go there and investigate the scene, preserve it and make sure it's done properly. We responded to it as if it were a murder with no suspect. There had been a murder; we needed to make sure that the man who shot himself was the only person involved, we had to make sure was he acting alone. Did he have friends? Were other firearms involved? Then we had to look into the background of him and the victim to see what had gone on before and to see what had caused this terrible event to happen

I had been in central London when I got the call, so I happened to get to Knightsbridge before a lot of my team, but I needed the normal sort of forensic work done as well as local enquiries.

When all the team arrived at Harvey Nichols, there was the immediate problem of where to have the briefing. Since we were all in the cosmetics department on the ground floor, where the incident had taken place, there were chairs where customers sit to get make-up applied by the staff, and we were able to use those. There was this slightly surreal scene of a murder squad sitting down on the make-up chairs with me behind the counter giving them the information. It was the most incongruous scene I ever did a briefing in.

What we were told by the eyewitnesses was that Clare Bernal was working as usual on the cosmetics counter, Pech had come into the store, he'd shot her, she had fallen to the floor and he turned the gun and shot himself in the head.

There had been at least three shots fired – two or possibly three fired at the victim and then the shooter used one on himself.

As soon as the incident happened, the store was evacuated. We kept it closed while we were doing our forensic work and enquiries and it was closed for a few days.

One of the issues we had was that we could only recover three bullets from the bodies of Clare and Pech – but we had four cartridge cases. We needed to find that fourth bullet.

At one point, I got a call from a senior executive at Harvey Nichols who asked when he could have his shop back. "It's costing us tens of thousands of pounds every hour we are shut," he said. I pointed out that his loyal and wealthy customers wouldn't be too impressed if they moved something on a shelf and found a bloody bullet behind it, He understood instantly, saying: "Mr Sutton, do what you need to do and tell me when we can re-open."

As my team carried on with the normal things that you do in the early hours of a homicide investigation – searches and forensic work – I knew that we were going to have to find out why a man who said he loved and cherished a young woman had walked into her place of work, brutally shot and murdered her and then killed himself. We had so many questions that needed answering, What was someone doing with a handgun in Harvey Nichols? Why did it come to this? And one which we needed to answer most quickly– was he acting alone?

There were two main initial lines of enquiry. First there was the relationship between Clare and Pech – we knew they had been seeing each other, how did that progress, what happened and had it caused him to react the way he did? Secondly we had to look at Pech and his associates, was he part of a gang? Were there further associates of his with firearms?

It transpired that Clare Bernal shouldn't have been working that evening, she had swapped shifts with her flatmate. As the story started unfolding and we realised the shooter, her ex-boyfriend Michael Pech, had gone to the store to find her, we assumed he must have gone to her home first because he would have expected her not to be at work. He worked for Harvey Nichols as a security officer, he had access to her rotas and shifts. There was the worry that if he had gone to the flat that she shared with a colleague, what had happened there? Might there be another victim lying dead in the flat in Dulwich, south London, where they lived? It became a priority for us to get down to Dulwich to check on the safety of Clare's co-worker.

We came to the flat, knocked on the door and got no answer. We were standing outside, debating whether there was a real risk, and if we should force entry, when a young lady in a tracksuit carrying a gym bag came along and sat on the wall just outside the entrance to the flat. She was talking on a mobile phone and, together with DI Tony McKeown, I went and approached her. By a strange coincidence, both Tony and I had learned some Russian at school and we glanced at each other when we both realised that was the language the young lady was speaking. Since we knew that was where Clare's friend Anna hailed from, we were instantly relieved.

"I'm sitting here because I can't get into the flat; I haven't got a key and I was waiting for Clare to come back with the key," she told us. Our relief then turned to sorrow as we had to break the news that Clare, her friend, colleague and flatmate, was dead. We had to arranged for Anna to spend the night somewhere because we couldn't get her into the flat without the keys. She was absolutely devastated that her friend and colleague had been murdered. We mentioned Pech and she told us that Clare moved here to get away from him, he had been harassing her, stalking her at her previous address. He had then found out that this was where she had moved to and he started the same thing at the Dulwich address. "He hung around here and would accost her on the way to and from work," Anna told us. Pech had eventually been arrested by the police on stalking charges. In fact he had been convicted and released on bail, pending sentence in a few weeks.

Having confirmed that Clare's flatmate was safe, we needed to find out more about Michael Pech. At that point we didn't know who he was, who his associates were. Was he a one-off? Was he a lone wolf? Was it only about Clare, or did he live or associate with a lot of people who were armed? Were there any more firearms and ammunition back where he lived?

We discovered he lived in a house in South Tottenham and again, while those on the team were doing what they could with the scene and witnesses at Harvey Nichols, Tony McKeown and I went to north London to his house. It was an end of terrace property, it was almost derelict. The grass was three feet high in the garden, a window or two broken and the front door was almost hanging off, when we got there. It was not in a good condition. It reminded me of the old cartoon Wacky Races. There was a car that had a chimney and bats flying around it there, a haunted house – the Creepy Coupé I think it was called. It was just like that, bathed in moonlight, with a door off its hinges, wide open, with broken windows. There were tiles missing off the roof and it creaked as you walked in. It was like a squat.

If you made a drama of it and featured the house as it was, people would think you were overplaying it. The occupants were, in the event completely benign and helpful, but you just looked at it and it seemed like something out of a different time or a different country. There were a few places like that in Tottenham, I'd worked as a community PC on the Broadwater Farm Estate. There'd be these 1930s semis or terraces and every now and then there'll be a detached house at the end. If you look at the pictures after the riots on Broadwater

Farm, there's a house like that, a detached one, that was completely burnt out, a prison officer lived there.

It was in the early hours of the morning and we had got a panda car from the local police station in Tottenham and were accompanied by a couple of uniformed police officers. Although we were going in there thinking we might be looking for firearms or people with firearms, we knew that we had no chance of getting armed backup. It was one of those situations where it was obviously dangerous – but it wasn't dangerous enough. We just knew we couldn't get that sort of backup – it happens quite often as a police officer. Tony and I sat there and looked at each other and said: "Well, we know it's not 100 per cent safe but 99 per cent of the time it will be, so come on let's do it."

We went in, armed with a torch, a mini-Maglite, that was all.

It was dark and creepy in the house, it was all very threadbare. There were actually seven men sleeping in the house that night. All of them were from Eastern Europe and all of them working on building sites. Pech had been the eighth man living there. One of the young men, a chap named Georg, was huge, about six feet eight inches tall. He was Polish and could speak very good English and he translated for the rest of them. He was really helpful, so much so he then took Tony and I to Earls Court and pointed out the hotel he knew Pech had been staying in once he got back from a trip abroad. We were able to search Pech's room in Tottenham, we found nothing, no more firearms. The next day, however, one of the newspapers reported that "armed police stormed a house in Tottenham". "More like police armed with a sense of humour and a biro stormed a house in Tottenham," Tony said.

Clare's friend was obviously devastated at the death of her friend but she started to tell us more about what had gone on in the relationship between Clare and Michael Pech. We came to realise there was an awful lot about this murder and suicide that we had yet to understand.

He had become very obsessive and very serious about their relationship extremely quickly. It wasn't what Clare wanted and she didn't really know how to deal with it. She'd had conversations with her friends and family explaining that this relationship was causing her difficulties because she felt it was all going too far, too fast and he wanted it to be much more serious than she did. And that was probably why for her, the relationship fizzled out.

But Pech was not the kind of man to take no for an answer.

He set upon a course of stalking her relentlessly, it became so bad that at one point she was receiving on average 50 texts or calls from him per day. She wasn't returning the calls or messages, she really didn't want to know. He would appear at her flat, he would appear at railway stations when he knew she was travelling to and from work. He was quite obviously obsessed.

Clare eventually felt that she had no choice but to take the appropriate action about the stalking that she was suffering.

The reaction of the management at Harvey Nichols was to make sure that Pech was deployed in a different part of the building. But he was still able to misuse the internal CCTV to see where Clare was and then to move around the shop to be close to her and to talk to her. This was in direct contravention of the instructions he had received from his management and he was warned about it, but when he persisted, he was eventually suspended.

And yet still, Pech continued his stalking behaviour. Clare became understandably disturbed when she heard that he had been asking around colleagues what the penalty for murder was in the UK. Eventually she had no choice but to go to the police and report him. Pech was actually arrested while he was at work at Harvey Nichols and at that point the management said: "Sorry, that's it, you're sacked." He was fired from the job.

The police took the report seriously, investigated it thoroughly and Pech was charged and had to appear at court. This was possibly the catalyst that tipped him over the edge, as he realised his dream of a relationship with Clare Bernal was never going to come true. He clearly took the clichéd view that if he couldn't have her, then nobody could.

Pech was a former soldier in the Czech Republic and he went back to the country of his birth. Having attended a proficiency course and got his licence, he quite lawfully purchased a firearm and ammunition. He then headed back to the UK on a coach via Dover and managed pass through security armed with this pistol and some rounds of ammunition hidden in a holdall. By now he was a very disappointed, frustrated, unstable man with an automatic pistol and ammunition. It was a tragedy waiting to happen; he'd obviously made the decision: "I'm going to kill her then I'm going to kill myself."

When Pech appeared at court on the harassment charge he pleaded guilty. Clare was quite relieved; his admission meant she wasn't called to give evidence against him. She thought the whole thing was over, that it was behind her. It was during the time he was on bail awaiting sentence that he went back and killed Clare and himself.

It was difficult to see any relevance in the fact he was given bail. Would he have received a custodial sentence for what he had done? The answer is almost certainly not, so the fact that he was on bail becomes irrelevant. Had he been sentenced immediately he would still have been free to undertake his deadly mission.

But what nobody expected was that he was going to take a large dose of cocaine, go into the store with an automatic pistol, murder her and kill himself.

I knew from the very start there would be a huge amount of media interest in this case because it was so unusual, and so tragic. As the story unfolded and as more became known about Clare and about Michael Pech and the court cases, it became clear it was not only tragic, but it was possibly avoidable.

At the time the response of law enforcement and of the courts to stalking as a crime – and a phenomenon in its own right – was in its infancy. There were measures you could take and there were offences he was committing, but it wasn't joined up in the way it is now. This had a bearing on this case, there is no doubt that given the way that Michael Pech had behaved, the warning signs were there that something like this might have happened. There was already a pretty good groundswell of lobbying by decent and sensible people about stalking.

One of the things I think Clare Bernal's case does highlight is the fact that the legal system isn't really equipped to deal with the quantum leap between stalking and murder. Pech was charged with stalking, he was taken to court and was on bail awaiting sentence when he killed her. People spoke harshly about it at the time, the implication being that he shouldn't have been bailed.

But you need to look at the offence, which he was quite clearly guilty of, and what the punishment was. There is no way that, even if he were sentenced on that day, he would have received a custodial sentence. Whatever happened that day in court, he was always going to walk out of the door there and then.

It's a really difficult area because assessing the risk of stalking escalating to murder is not an exact science, there's always a degree of subjectivity, there's always the possibility for error, for the scope not being correct and for not everything being taken into account. There's no foolproof way of saying "this stalker is going to become a murderer in two weeks, so let's deal with it".

That's where the pressure and the whole movement to criminalise stalking – with which I agree – falls down. You can't incarcerate stalkers and you can't tell which stalker is going to become the murderer. You can try your best to but it's not going to be foolproof even if it works 50 per cent of the time. It's the same with missing persons – how do you know which missing person is going to be the one that ends up dead? You can have all the protocols, algorithms and flowcharts in the world but they're never foolproof. A young trainee detective I was speaking to told me she had 124 cases of domestic abuse that she was dealing with, live cases – yes, that was the caseload of just one officer. And she asked: "How do I tell which one's going to be the murderer?"

"You can't," I replied.

There are clues, there are risk assessment matrices and guidance but at the end of the day, you can't be certain which one's going to be right. There's still an air of unpredictability. It's really unfair to criticise and judge police or social services or whoever's involved in that risk assessment process. Even if they've done the very best they can, they're still never going to achieve absolute certainty.

Clare's mother Patricia used the tragedy to the best effect she could by making herself an advocate for victims of stalking and becoming a voice and part of the pressure on the government to change the law and to give the courts and police more powers when dealing with these offences. One must never lose sight of the fact they are trying to protect often vulnerable young women from unwanted attention from men. I would say the media were very helpful in that too because they saw the issue, that it was a chance to do some real good and make a difference so women in the future would be less likely to suffer in the way Clare did.

I think it shows how we do things on The Real Manhunter. We always contact the family and I spoke to Clare's mother Tricia and initially, she wasn't keen to get involved.

I'd had something to do with her at the time of the case, but not a huge amount. I knew she was a nice, well-educated and very reasonable lady who had suffered greatly. I ended up having a Zoom meeting with her before we made it – it was during lockdown. I broached the subject with her. I said they had a specific story to tell – like the Donovans, Christopher's parents, you've turned this tragedy into a force for good by forming a charity aimed at preventing stalking and dealing with stalking.

I said she should take this as an opportunity to get some free publicity for her campaign and talk about it to us. I promised her we wouldn't cut it out, I said she could talk to us about the charity and what they do as much as they liked, because it's part of the story.

I later had another Zoom with her and the person who's the chief executive of her charity and they agreed. It was a really powerful programme in the end. It underlines the fact that Revelation, the production company behind The Real Manhunter and myself haven't got an agenda – we'll go where the case takes us.

We want to support these people who have suffered and people who have had to deal with these things happening to them and where there's an opportunity to get them to talk about something like that, then we're happy to give it to them. She took advantage of it and I think it was a really powerful part of it. I'm not a TV person obviously, but I wonder whether there would be many production companies who would be that willing to effectively give over a quarter of a programme for someone to bang a drum about a charity. I'm quite proud we did that because it still made a really good episode. I've had experience of working for other companies I'm not sure they'd do the same thing. I think it was the right thing to do and I think it worked really well.

It was all so sad – this very attractive 22-year-old girl who really loved her job. It's difficult to understand how somebody could react to rejection by somebody they thought they loved and wanted to be with in that way, by killing that person. It happens and we know it happens, but it doesn't make it easier to understand how someone can act like that.

CHAPTER 9
THE MURDER OF ALLAN CHAPPELOW

The Bellfield investigation was still running in 2006. It took up every waking moment really, apart from when we were on call or we were given a new case.

In June 2006 we had recently – just a couple of months previously – charged Levi Bellfield with the murder offences for which he was going to stand trial. We were very much involved in preparing that case, but we were having to take our share of doing on call work and indeed other investigations.

I still had more DIs than usual on the team and when we took on relatively simple cases, I could oversee those and allow one of them to take the lead. It enabled us to manage the workload, indeed for me to manage mine – there were so many documents for me to read and sign off, more than 65,000 in the Bellfield case alone. But it also meant the DIs and DSs were given the opportunity to extend their experience and hone their skills.

By the time we finished the Bellfield case, I had an extremely capable set of supervisors in terms of the

DIs and the DSs on my team. They'd all been through so much and had gained such valuable experience.

So much of the Bellfield investigation wasn't driven by forensics, it wasn't driven by science, because we had none. Once you'd dealt with the CCTV and dealt with the sort of analysis of the telecommunications data, everything else was knocking on doors, taking statements off people. I feel a bit of a fraud when I say it was an old-fashioned investigation because it was so reliant on CCTV. But if you take that away, there was an awful lot of old-fashioned detective work. It was all about taking little bits of information from here and there and putting them into the database Eventually they piled up together and made a compelling case.

I don't believe Bellfield took a great toll on me at all. I was pretty apprehensive when it very first started, because I realised straight away how important it was. Part of that was the idea that he was going to keep doing this until we caught him. You read it in novels and you see it on dramas, but it was really a case of how long did we have until he killed another one? When you live that for real and it's real people on the other end of it, it's quite a scary thing. That aspect was huge and I probably worked more hours than I would otherwise have done, but I don't think it took a physical or mental toll. I mean, I enjoyed it to a certain extent. If you're an actor, then you want to be in the biggest Hollywood movies, or you want to be on stage at the National Theatre. If you're a runner, you want to be at the Olympics, in the final. If you're an SIO, you want to solve a serial murder case.

I actually did two different kinds of training to become an SIO; I was trained by the old modular system and then as I was (unusually) still performing the role years later I also went through the PIP3 process. Some SIOs were further trained to do serious and serial investigations and I was one of them. Of those who pass that extra course there is quite a small percentage, maybe five per cent or so who actually get to lead such an investigation for real. This is because, happily, there are so few serial or serious cases. Somehow I ended up being SIO in two major serious investigations, which is very unusual.

There was a degree of jealousy, there were a lot of people who wished that they could have done the Bellfield case but I don't imagine many envied me taking over the Night Stalker. I didn't really care what people thought of me then; or what people think of me now, pretty much. But I'd go to meetings, tasking meetings and the like, where people would discuss what investigations they were leading.

I heard first behind my back and then to my face people call me a "one-job" – Colin "One-Job" Sutton. At the time, we had people covering for the on-call and we were never in the frame for a new job. In 2005 we had a command day as they used to call it, like a training day for the SIOs and their deputies. I asked if I could have a half-hour slot, to update people on what we were doing with Bellfield, what it was like doing it. I worked out by then we were investigating 27 concurrent serious offences – and they were calling me one job! I went through it all and told them, showed them exactly what we were doing and then as I showed the last slide of my presentation, I said: "I've only got this one job at the moment so you're quite right to call me that."

It was the best thing I could have done because my colleagues there started coming and saying: “I can't believe it, I didn't realise what you and your team were doing.” But although that stopped the sniping, I think it actually made more people realise: "Shit, I wish I could do that, I wish I was on that one case.”

The Bellfield workload only ever became a problem if we had some sort of big event – if we were having him out from prison to interview him, or we had searches or arrests or something like that. Otherwise it was workable, you have to put something down and pick something else up.

To be honest, we were used to doing that, that's what the murder team was. Even if we did have something like Bellfield going on, we took other cases on. We did half a dozen category B cases – reasonably difficult cases. If we'd not had Bellfield, we'd have probably taken on twice as many. There was always a kind of tacit understanding that we had a lot going on with Bellfield. that our capacity wasn't huge, but that we could do some cases. In truth I think it kept the team fresh, it stopped us going stale because you're only doing one thing.

Most murder teams would have four or five of their constables trying to do disclosure for the defence, marking up whether it's relevant or not. There were times when we were doing disclosure for the defence, we had every single officer on the team from sergeant and constable rank trying to do it. I got £20,000 from the central overtime budget as a bonus to pay overtime to do disclosure, which is unheard of – you don't pay overtime for doing disclosure. We had to fit in with the schedule that the court had given us and to do that we had to do disclosure on 300 documents a week for three months or we'd fall behind. There's a limit to the amount of time you can sit in front of a screen clicking before you're not concentrating and you're not doing it properly. The defence would be looking for anything they could catch you out on, saying we hadn't done this bit properly, so it doesn't count, it's not admissible.

This is the kind of thing his legal team were looking for, something that could prejudice the trial, anything they could catch us out on. I spent five and a half months at court thinking "is this going be the day when that comes up?", and it never did. You can't be absolutely certain, but I was pretty confident we'd done it properly.

The trial was set for February 2007 and Louise and I went on holiday. I was sitting by the pool and got a call from Jo Brunt to say the trial had been postponed – it was meant to be starting about a week after I got back.

"Oh, for God's sake," I said. "Why is that?"

The defence had gone to court and said: "There's quite a lot to read here isn't there?"

It was as if they had only just realised that. It was put off for eight months. It actually started in October. If the defence had realised that earlier, our disclosure timetable would have been a lot slacker, because we were trying to get ready for February.

Then the interesting thing was that, how do you do it? The defence has a right to look at the unused material – if we say it's not relevant, they've still got a right to look at it. They wanted to see our unused material, so they had to come to Putney. We used part of our conference room and they sent about six or eight trainee solicitors, all with shiny new MacBook Airs. They came in and they sat down with the list and said: "Right, can we see this document?"

They'd go off and get the document. After about three days DC Jayne Farnworth, who was liaising with them, came to me and said the solicitors kept asking for the same thing. Of the six of them, four had asked for the same document.

I told Jayne to give them exactly what they asked for. It wasn't our place to try to tell them how to do their job. And if they ask for the same document every day for the next six weeks, we would give them it. And that's what we did. It was like when you arrest somebody for possession of drugs – you go back to their home address and do a search. If you've not got somebody who takes hold of that, the bookcase gets searched three times while nobody looks in the cupboard under the stairs. They didn't have a plan, they didn't have a strategy. They were just these youngsters sent in there, just having a look. It wasn't our job to organise how they prepared their defence.

In June 2006, and as well as working on Bellfield, we were on call for a week, and we got a request to respond from the police at Hampstead who had a bit of a mystery case.

They'd had a report that a man who lived in a very expensive house in Hampstead hadn't been seen for a number of days and it was brought to their attention not by a friend or family, as would normally be the case, but by a financial institution. HSBC told police that there was unusual activity on his bank account involving transfers, a strange pattern of transactions. He'd started to use internet banking which he hadn't done before and they feared the worst – he'd not been seen and staff had not been able to contact him to try and verify these events.

It's one of those calls that you get where on one end of the spectrum, some SIOs might simply say: "Very interesting, but phone me back when you've found that there is a murder." And perhaps I was more to the other end of the spectrum whereby if we had the time and resources to help, then I thought it was our duty and our job to see what we could do. It was kind of a cross between a welfare check and whether something untoward had happened.

Hampstead was part of our patch that we didn't go to very often. It's a very wealthy area, just yards from Hampstead Heath. The scene was a house in Downshire Hill which runs down from the police station to the Heath. When we got there, there was a stark contrast between the surroundings and the beautiful, very valuable homes and the one that we went to. Although it had clearly once been one of them, it had been left in a shocking state of disrepair. Rubbish, machinery, motorbikes, washing machines littered the front garden, so much detritus we could barely get into the premises. But we were told that that's where Allan Chappelow lived and he was missing, he had been missing for several weeks.

The local police had been there and had a look and tried to search the premises the best they could, but because of the state of it, they called us in. There were literally millions and millions of sheets of paper in piles inside the house, bags of rubbish, complete chaos. It looked like Allan Chappelow never threw anything away. The local officers realised that trying to conduct a proper search for that house in that condition was going to be beyond their limited resources and so they called for some help.

Allan Chappelow was a photographer, primarily. He was almost an obsessive fan of George Bernard Shaw and had, late in the writer's life, been granted a meeting with him where he eventually persuaded the great author to be photographed. One of those photographs he took has become more or less the definitive picture of Shaw and is now in the National Portrait Gallery.

But Allan Chappelow had other interests too. He wanted to be a literary agent, or involved with authors and he collected manuscripts. When I say collected, that doesn't do his accumulation justice – there were millions of pages, all around his house. When we went there to look, it was clear that he was somewhat of a recluse. He didn't really have any local friends and led a relatively simple life, but it seems everything he ever bought or possessed he kept. This very expensive property in a very desirable road was in a state of virtual disrepair. There was filth and muck and detritus and debris everywhere; there were a couple of motorcycles in the house; it hadn't had any maintenance for a long time and the garden was full of rusty tools, wheelbarrows, yet another motorcycle and boxes and bags of rubbish.

I decided that we ought to search the house, we went in to make a start and really found that doing it by hand was virtually impossible. But to be honest, by now my interest in this case had been well and truly aroused. It really was a mystery and the sort of mystery that I like to get to the bottom of if I can.

Before we could start searching, before we even went in to do it, I wanted to know what the strength of the information was. It would seem that he was a man who possessed neither a computer nor smart phone, but yet had recently signed up for online banking. The records for this showed that he was making payments to a couple of recipients that couldn't easily be explained. They weren't companies or business accounts, just individuals. And his cash was frequently being withdrawn from ATMs. It looked suspicious and when you tie that information in with his lifestyle there was something of a mismatch. It all simply didn't add up.

The house itself had big rooms, with high ceilings, but some of them we just physically couldn't get into. Somebody estimated there were around 4 million individual sheets of A4 paper in that house. It was one of the most bizarre crime scenes I ever saw.

Once inside, one of the difficulties we had was actually what to do with all this debris and paper that we had to move. The front garden of the house was full of rubbish as well and needed to be searched. In the end, we had to cordon off half of the road and erect a scenes of crime tent within that on the roadway. We had to then move the rubbish and materials out from the house into that area to sift through, it wasn't possible to do it inside the house.

As we started moving things, as we could see more of what was happening in the house it was just remarkable. There were trees that had been growing up through the floorboards. When we looked more closely at the roof, we found that missing tiles had been replaced by supermarket plastic carrier bags that had been stuck where the tiles should be. It was the most remarkable scene of dereliction and decrepitude.

There were a couple of rooms where there was so much paper piled high which in turn had been knocked over, that you'd literally open the door and find a sea of paper four or five feet high. Searching for something even the size of a human body in there was going to be really difficult there and then. We had a choice: Either get sufficient staff and officers down there to dig all of this paper and detritus out of the house - or would we be able to shortcut it by using a dog?

A police dog and her handler were sent along to help us, it was a German Shepherd named Lacey. Lacey went in and had a run around as best she could in the house and there was one particular room where she alerted really strongly, by barking and pawing at the paper in the room, and I spoke to the handler and he said: "There's something in there that she's found very interesting."

I said: "OK, we'll bite the bullet and clear that room."

And it was in that room, under these piles of paper that we found the body of Allan Chappelow. He was in a really bad way, he was in a kind of foetal position under this paper and he had injuries to his head and to his chest. There had been quite a bit of decomposition, we couldn't tell immediately how long he had been there but it was obvious he'd been there for some period.

It was about as suspicious a death as you could get, and so that was the point where we knew we had a murder investigation on our hands.

The postmortem examination of Allan Chappelow's body showed that he had probably been strangled, he had a lot of broken bones around his neck. The top half of his body, quite bizarrely, was covered with congealed wax and burn marks. The implication there was that there had been some sort of torture, or some sort of violent heat from burning objects applied to him while he was still alive. He was so decomposed that to try to ascertain how long he had been dead, the services of specialist scientists who look at blowflies and maggots and their incubation were called upon. They used the stage of development of insects to make an assessment of how long the body had lain there.

It took the detectives some time to try to unravel what had happened. Allan Chappelow had numerous bank accounts, he had a share portfolio and just prior to his being found dead, somebody had set up online access to his accounts. Since he didn't have a computer, it was clear that somebody wasn't him. A PIN had been posted to his house which would enable him to use this online banking and move money about; it had clearly been received by somebody because it had been used and money withdrawn.

Most of the money seemed to be moved not to a business or an organisation but to an account the reference was just titled "Money TT, Ref: Jenny". The locations for these internet transactions did move about but seemed to be focused upon an internet café somewhere in Charing Cross, which again was not something we could imagine that Chappelow would have done himself.

The real breakthrough came when information was received that Allan Chappelow's Sainsbury's credit card had been used at an Indian restaurant not very far from his house in Hampstead. That gave officers somewhere to go to, to speak to staff with the hope there might be CCTV inside the premises. They were very helpful because they remembered this transaction or attempted transaction. They said it was an East Asian man who'd tried to pay with his credit card but it had been declined. He had, in turn, tried to phone the bank to get them to release it, to unlock the card so he could use it. He failed in this but during that conversation he told them his name was Allan. Allan Chappelow could by no stretch of the imagination be described as an East Asian man in his 40s, which was the description the staff in the restaurant gave.

The man calling himself Allan and his female companion agreed with the staff that they would leave the man's mobile phone there as a kind of security and they would come back then with money or with a working card and settle the bill.

Staff at the restaurant remembered the man used a silver flip type phone to make a phone call to his bank. That's important because we did know that Allan Chappelow did possess a mobile phone but it was a very simple black Nokia phone and not a flip type. The bank use the SIM card as part of the verification procedure when you try to do telephone banking with them. Somehow Allan Chappelow's SIM card had found its way into this man's silver flip phone.

You'd think somebody who knew enough about accessing bank accounts - who would know to take the original SIM and use that to contact the bank – was a person who was practised in fraud and deception. From an investigative point of view, the crucial thing is that when SIM cards are moved from one handset to another and they communicate with the network, they also tell the network the serial number, known as the IMEI, of the handset they are in.

The IMEI number identifies that handset as unique in the world. So, officers at the telephone information unit at Scotland Yard can go to the mobile phone providers and say: "Ok, on this date for this telephone call, which handset was this SIM card in?" and that again is a potential line of enquiry that could lead us to the actual individual.

The female companion eventually came back to the restaurant, she did retrieve the phone because she paid for the bill, partially in cash and partially with a credit card. The staff told the police that she'd even left them a £2 tip. The tip for the police was even better – she'd used her own credit card and that gave a trail back to her real identity.

I think it's fair to assume that this woman had no idea what the mysterious Asian man calling himself Allan was doing. If she had known that he was there trying to use a murdered man's credit card, she would realise how foolish it would be for her to use her own credit card there and supply this trail back to a real person.

Police were able to identify her credit card issuer and ask them if there were any other recent transactions and they told them that the last transaction that she had made on the card was to buy an air ticket to Zurich.

It was too late to stop the flight, she'd already flown to Zurich, but what it did give was the opportunity to go to the airport to look at CCTV, to see what she looked like, who she was, and if she was with anybody else while she was travelling.

Meanwhile, the information came back from Scotland Yard: the mobile phone providers had confirmed the silver flip phone was registered to a man who lived in Denning Road, Belsize Park, not too far from the scene.

Police went to the address and found that it was a rented house. The landlady took great care and pride in vetting her tenants very thoroughly before she let the room to them. On this occasion, however, she had been desperate to fill the room because she was short of money so she perhaps hadn't gone as deeply into the background of her tenant as she'd have liked to. He was a man called Wang Yam.

The investigation then moved on to Wang Yam. He was a Chinese dissident who had graduated in computer science. He had left China in 1991 and applied for asylum in the UK. He settled in this country and he went into business, but it turned out he was a pretty terrible businessman. He went bankrupt on two separate occasions and had total debts in excess of £1.1 million pounds

Wang Yam was in a financial predicament and he was looking at a number of ways to extricate himself. I think it's possible he was attracted to Chappelow's house because it was so derelict; maybe he thought nobody lived there.

At some point in spring 2006, Allan Chappelow had, quite unusually, gone on holiday to America, leaving the house unoccupied. It appears that at this time, Wang Yam decided to start dipping through the letter box and seeing if he could pick up the mail that was arriving there, to try to turn it to his financial advantage some way. It was during the period while Allan Chappelow was away that the breach of his financial details and his bank account occurred. It was when Wang Yam set up the internet banking and started making the transfers, effectively stealing Chappelow's money.

Early in May 2006, Allan Chappelow came back from America. We don't know for certain, but it's a good theory that at some point, Wang Yam went to the house to dip some more mail from the letter box and found Allan Chappelow there. It could have been that the meeting between the two was accidental and unplanned, but by then Wang Yam had obviously got a really good idea of how much Allan Chappelow was worth, as he had access to all his bank accounts. This was a golden goose and as far as Wang Yam was concerned, it was going to keep giving.

The type of fraud that Wang Yam had conducted here is known as a "facility takeover", essentially he is impersonating the holder of the accounts and gaining access to the money in those accounts by pretending to be that person and using online and telephone banking. Wang Yam had found a way to solve his financial difficulties, he knew that there was a lot of money there available to him and he would keep this going.

When Allan Chappelow came home from his holiday and Wang Yam was confronted with him, he feared this line of funds was about to disappear. That fear then caused him to turn from fraud to murder.

Had Allan Chappelow not returned or even after he returned and was murdered, I suspect Wang Yam's long-term aim was to sell the house. He knew that despite its condition it was very valuable.

By the time we discovered all this, Wang was in Switzerland with Dong Hui, but by September 2006, three or four months after Allan Chappelow was murdered, the Swiss police detained him and he was extradited back to Britain to face charges of murder, theft and fraud.

Wang claimed – and it was later substantiated – he had been acting as an informant for MI6, Britain's foreign intelligence service. He was probably well placed to be an informant for the security services, his family were long time dissidents in China, and he was something of a computer expert.

When Wang Yam's trial began in 2008, there was a remarkable piece of British judicial history, it was the first time in modern times that a court had been cleared and a murder trial was to take place without any members of the public present and with no reporting. This was due to an application made by the security services that to do so would harm their tactics and techniques and would expose matters of national security to the public eye.

Wang Yam pleaded guilty to the fraud charges, but not guilty to the murder charges. The case in his defence was that he had been working for MI6, and had been passing information on to what he called, "the appropriate authorities".

The prosecution case was that he had repeatedly gone to Allan Chappelow's house, dipping through the letter box to retrieve letters and PIN numbers from the bank, that he had on one occasion confronted him and it was during that confrontation that Allan Chappelow was murdered. There was also some conjecture that also because of the scale of his debts, £1.1 million pounds, that his further plan would have been to try to sell Allan Chappelow's house and realise a huge sum.

At his first trial, the jury couldn't agree on that murder charge, so there was another trial. At the second trial, he was found guilty of murdering Allan Chappelow. The judge recommended he serve at least 20 years before he would be eligible to apply for parole.

In 2018, Allan Chappelow's neighbour, Thomas Harding, published a book called Blood On The Page, which cast some doubt over the safety of the conviction of Wang Yam for his murder. Harding suggested that there was no physical evidence linking him to the murder scene or to Allan Chappelow's body and indeed at this time there had been a spate of these dipping thefts through letter boxes in the general area of the house.

I think to do so ignores the fact that the financial evidence was very strong, whoever had killed Allan Chappelow had the confidence to go and use his phone, his credit card and his SIM card in a restaurant 100 yards away, knowing that he wouldn't walk through the door at any moment.

If you think about it, there is really no other explanation. Wang Yam must have been there, must've been dipping through that letterbox to get possession of the bank cards, probably had been inside the house to get the SIM card and if there is another set of circumstances like, for example, "well someone else has stolen them and given them or sold them to me", then that's what Wang Yam would have said, wouldn't he, in his defence? Pleading guilty to a relatively minor offence of handling stolen goods and fraud is far preferable to allowing yourself to be convicted of murder.

Even in this appalling condition of disrepair and filth, the house was still worth £4 million. Allan Chappelow had died intestate, there was no will, so police had quite a job on their hands to trace Allan's relatives who should be inheriting this estate. The new owners very quickly put in planning applications to restore it to its former glory, it gives an indication of the value of the house and location that even somewhere as broken down and derelict as this was sold for more than £4 million.

Finding the people to whom the house would pass was a very difficult job for lawyers and HMRC, they were looking for next of kin and family members over here and eventually the proceeds from the house sale actually went to family members in Denmark, because they were the closest family that could be found.

CHAPTER 10
THE MURDER OF MIRIAM BALDOCK & ATTEMPTED MURDER OF MAURICE BALDOCK

The Bellfield trial took place from October 2007 to February 2008.

I don't think it ever took a toll on me. It's something people have asked me a lot and it's possibly an unsatisfactory explanation I give. But I learned very quickly when I joined the police, policing generally, that there was a whole world out there with people who lived their lives in a very different way from what I was accustomed to. I had to accept that and accept that it was part of my job to be professional and deal with them and their lives.

When I joined the police I lived in Enfield and was stationed in Tottenham and it's only a few miles down the road, but in that distance there was a world of difference. I looked at a few things open-mouthed at first, but you had to accept that this is the other side of the job and that's what you do. I was always able to be professional and deal with what was in front of me.

Yes, of course, on occasions you'd say this is bloody tragic. But there's a realisation you come to quite quickly that when tragic things happen someone has got to step in and deal, and it is your job to do it.

In August 2007 we were the on-call team for west London murder. It was just six weeks before the Bellfield trial started and we were up to our neck in that, doing disclosure and no person was more busy at that than Jo Brunt. Then we got the call to attend a flat in Camden.

The first report was that one person, a woman, had died and that a man was seriously injured. It was obviously going to be a murder investigation, and we were just hoping at that point there was going to be just one victim rather than two.

When we arrived it was a usual scene around a suspected murder, slightly complicated by the fact that there had been a lot of activity by the paramedics who had tried to intervene. It was a horrific sight.

We found out that the man, who was called Maurice Baldock, had sustained three horrible knife wounds to his chest, he'd been taken away to hospital and was literally clinging to life. His wife, Miriam, sadly was dead. The couple, in their 60s, had been brutally stabbed in their own home. The fact they'd been attacked while they were lying in their bed gave it a greater dimension of horror. The idea that this couple could have just been peacefully sleeping together in their bed, and were then attacked, with one of them was dead and the other nearly dead, made it seem a terrible crime from the very start.

One of the things we were keen to work out at the start of the investigation was whether this was a random crime as the result of a burglary or some attempt of theft in the flat, or whether it was an assault targeted on this couple.

There were no signs of forced entry at the flat, nor any indication there had been a search or indeed any valuable property missing. From the very beginning, it looked more like it was an attack targeted at this couple, but that begged the question – why? What could they have done, what could they have been involved in that would cause somebody to react in that way and attack them?

Maurice and Miriam Baldock were in the later stage of middle age I suppose, just into their 60s.

Throughout their life, they'd been devoted to caring for people, they'd fostered many, many children. They involved themselves greatly in the local area, they were very much part of a vibrant community around Maiden Lane where they lived. When we spoke to the neighbours, it showed how much regard they were held in. There was a genuine warmth of feeling for these people. More than one local described them as the "nicest people on the estate". It was a very nice, well-kept estate and they'd been instrumental in building up the community centre for the youths on the estate, they'd been foster parents over many years and they were just genuinely helpful, selfless people.

The more we found out about the Baldocks, the more tragic this all seemed, because they were people who had been the beating heart of their community.

That really made us even more bemused as to why they had become the target of a murderous knife attack in their own home, in their own bed? What could they have done and what could they have been involved in that would cause somebody to react in that way and attack them?

Although we had to carry on doing the usual forensic and scientific searches and evidence retrieval at the scene, it wasn't very long before we knew who our prime suspect was. The attention really for the squad was to then focus for the moment on trying to find him.

It emerged that there was no forced entry into the flat, it was obviously someone who had let themselves in with a key, it didn't take us long to work out that this was probably Stuart Forsyth, an ex-soldier.

He was from Scotland, from Lanarkshire originally, had been in the British Army and then, on leaving the forces, he served for a short while with the French Foreign Legion. It seems that as a result of his experiences as a soldier, that he was suffering from some sort of post-traumatic stress or a similar disorder.

It wasn't directly through their work as foster carers and child carers that the couple came into contact with Forsyth, however their attitudes, their desire to look after others and care for others in need, was very instrumental in how they met him and how they struck up a friendship with him.

They'd been in a pub one night and Stuart Forsyth happened to be there too. They didn't know him, but a car had backfired nearby which sent him into shock – he was really disturbed by this and hid under a table while many in the pub either ignored it or thought it was amusing.

Miriam and Maurice Baldock went over to try and help him, to see what was wrong with him and see what the matter was and their caring instinct sort of kicked in and not only did they look after him that night, but essentially he became one of their family. He was a regular visitor to their flat, he had a key to the premises, he introduced them to his daughter and despite his own difficulties with life as time went on as he battled abuse of both drugs and alcohol, the Baldocks were there as a constant in his life. They were always trying to keep him on the straight and narrow and to support him.

Once we'd got Stuart Forsyth's name, we were able to look into his contacts, his associates and the places he frequented. He had this mistaken belief that the Baldocks, despite all the love and care they'd shown him, thought he wasn't a fit and proper person to be looking after his daughter, and he'd convinced himself that they were going to try and have his daughter taken away from him and into care.

Nothing could have been further from the truth. What the Baldocks wanted to do was to try to support him and help him be the father he wanted to be to his daughter. But nevertheless, a degree of paranoia had taken hold in his mind and this had resulted in his attacking them.

We wanted to check on social workers and youth workers, people and agencies who would have been involved in his family care situation, just in case they too were at risk of an attack from him.

But all of that would be solved if we could just lay hands on him, the best way to ensure everybody's safety would be to arrest him.

Because we were able to speak to a number of Stuart Forsyth's friends and acquaintances and even members of the Baldock family, we got a pretty good idea of where he was likely to go. By the early half of the evening of that day we had a few addresses that could be visited.

Forsyth was nowhere to be found and I had the difficulty that we were on call, it was the weekend and there were other parts of the team who were dealing with other cases, all set against the background of preparing for this mammoth trial in just a few weeks. I relied heavily on Jo Brunt and DS Kevin McSharry to really keep the momentum going in this investigation. It was just a question of finding where Stuart Forsyth was. It was a true manhunt.

We were a bit short handed and thin on the ground and it ended up with myself and Jo Brunt, going to check out some of these addresses to see if we could find out where he was.

The first place we were sent to was a nightclub in Camden Town. We got there just as it was opening and there was a queue of people outside. It was some sort of speciality night – a fetish night – and there was a long queue of rather strangely dressed people waiting to go in. There were people in PVC, latex, rubber and chains and all sorts. I barged my way to the front of the queue in my suit – Jo had refused point blank to go in there, which was understandable. I banged on the door and said: "I'm police and I need to speak to the people in here."

I got in, spoke to the manager – when he asked me what I wanted I said: "I'm the band for the night." He looked me up and down and asked if I was having a laugh. I told him I was!

I explained who I was looking for, and they did know Stuart from other nights, from when the club had different events on, but certainly he wasn't there and they took my number and said they'd get in touch if he appeared.

And then we went to another club, a bikers' bar in Bethnal Green and we had a similar result there, no-one had seen Stuart for a few days.

It's strange, when you're wearing the uniform, it's obvious you're a police officer. Wearing a suit in places like that is just as good as wearing a uniform because they just look and realise you're not just a punter here. You must have some purpose.

It's perhaps interesting to reflect that the sort of places we were sent to try and find Stuart Forsyth, the kind of venues where he was known – a minority interest, almost fetish club in Camden, and a bikers' bar in Bethnal Green. Perhaps from that, we can tell that the sort of alternative lifestyles he'd fallen into or was interested in at that time. I think there's no doubt that he was somebody whose life experiences had a big effect on him, and his thinking, and his priorities at that time were pretty confused it seemed.

There was no trace of him at the last place he was known to have slept, but it was a bit difficult because he didn't really have a fixed address. It was obvious that he'd fled. We did know that he had a car, but we found the car and that was abandoned. We had no knowledge of his mobile phone, we couldn't use that to track him. We were settling in for what might have been a long hunt.

Don't forget this was a man who was born in Scotland, had been in the army and had been in the French

Foreign Legion, he'd travelled extensively and had few, if any, roots or ties to the London area. By this time, we were getting on for about 18 hours after the offence. That is a long time, during which a fugitive could easily get a very long way away.

It was one of those rare cases where I sought authority to release his name and pictures to the media, so that everybody else could help us and try to find him.

One of the main things you need to take into consideration when you're thinking of going public with a suspect's name like this is whether identification of him is going to be an issue further down the line. You need to be pretty much convinced you've got the right man before you set the whole of the media and effectively the general public out looking for him for you. We were so certain that he was going to be our man that the dangers to any identification procedures were minimal. We had no doubt that he was our murderer so we could take that step.

One of the other things I had to consider – was Stuart Forsyth a danger to other people? While we knew that there had been this connection between him and the Baldocks, and that was probably the motivation for what he had done, when someone is prepared to offer that extreme violence to people that he knows, you do wonder whether there's a possibility that he will offer it to others he doesn't know. So, there was always this danger that he is going to carry on his spree, and that was again another factor to be taken into consideration when we were thinking about whether to go public and to name him.

It seemed the best thing to do was to go to the public and say: "This is the man we need to speak to urgently in connection to this attack, if you see him please call the police and if you see him, don't approach him because he's used extreme violence against two other people already." We had to do all we could to keep the public safe.

We put his details into the media so we could get these thousands of pairs of eyes and ears of the public to try to help us to find him, I think it was probably that pressure that we applied to him that led him to surrender himself to a police officer.

As it turned out, he hitchhiked, he had thumbed a lift a number of times, each leg of his journey taking him further from the scene of his crime. We don't know whether he was just getting away from London aimlessly or if he was going somewhere he had in mind. I think it's probable that he was going wherever somebody would take him, because he ended up in Cornwall, and that wasn't an area where he had any particular reason to visit or had friends, family or history.

Whether the enormity of what he'd done was then weighing on his shoulders or whether he'd not been able to get alcohol and drugs for some time, and was perhaps sobering up and thinking more clearly, we will never know. But for whatever reason, he approached a police officer that he saw and said to the police officer: "I think you're probably looking for me, I've done something really bad."

It was not the ideal situation for us to have a prisoner to collect in Cornwall, because from there to London was quite a torturous and long journey. It was perhaps fortunate that the timing was such that we were still on call, which meant I had what's known as the "HAT car", the Homicide Assessment Team which is the crew that does night duty with a fast car, marked car, ready to deploy to suspicious deaths. We worked out that if I took them out of their response role and got cover from other areas, I could send the HAT car down to Cornwall and back in one journey, an overnight run to the far south west and back. So that's what we did.

Two officers went down to Cornwall to very quickly pick Forsyth up and brought him straight back to London, so by the time the rest of the team came back on duty the following morning, our prisoner was there in the cells waiting to be interviewed.

When Stuart Forsyth was spoken to by officers and what he'd done was put to him, he didn't admit it outright, but he spoke to the officers and said, yes, he knew what they were talking about and he knew the acts they were talking about but to him, it was something he had dreamt about. He said to him it felt like a bad dream that he'd attacked the Baldocks, but he hadn't actually done it.

The interviews progressed, with him just saying: "Yes, I dreamt it all." There was ample evidence with which to charge him with the murder of Miriam Baldock and the attempted murder of Maurice Baldock and that's what he was charged with and that's what he appeared in court for.

Stuart Forsyth readily admitted the stabbings and he subsequently appeared at the Old Bailey in February 2008. It was slightly unusual in these cases to admit to this kind of crime. I say, slightly unusual, because generally people who have committed these crimes know if they plead guilty, they are going to get a life sentence and there is no real incentive for them to not fight and at least give it a try. Perhaps a measure, perhaps an indication of some sort of remorse or regret that Stuart Forsyth felt, he took his punishment like a man; he held his hands up and pleaded guilty.

He was sentenced to life imprisonment and the judge's recommendation was that he should serve at least 19 years before being eligible to apply for parole.

The judge, Martin Stevens said: "Nothing can begin to excuse or explain the enormity of your actions. For many years, Miriam and Maurice Baldock treated you as their own son, they gave you nothing but kindness and support. And when in due course you had your own children, they treated them as their own grandchildren."

The 19-year term before he could apply for parole is perhaps slightly less than you'd expect for such a crime or such crimes, I think a number of things that fed into that.

One was the guilty plea, some credit is given for admitting the crime, but also the PTSD, I think that was a real issue and an important factor. When Stuart Forsyth's lawyers were mitigating for him, they alluded to this PTSD and said: "He did serve his country and he'd been serving and had been affected in this way." They also mentioned the fact that he was abusing alcohol and drugs at the time, and although that might be an explanation, it's not really something judges take much into account when they are sentencing, because they generally view it as an individual choice I suppose, whereas PTSD is not. Overall, I guess the 19 years is probably about right and what we expected.

There were certainly some people, some members of my team in fact, who thought the 19-year sentence he got was too lenient. I think sentencing is something more restricted by rules and precedents than most people realise and at that time too, the focus on knife crime generally wasn't as we see it now. It's quite possible that if this case were to come back anew before the courts now, that the recommendation would have been substantially longer.

Stuart Forsyth is still serving his term of imprisonment, it will be February 2027 before he can apply for parole. We don't really know what's gone on since he's been in prison, but he's certainly been involved in an altercation with another prisoner while there and he himself was stabbed.

The case of Stuart Forsyth and the attacks on Miriam and Maurice Baldock, is interesting in some ways because it's one of those cases that sadly somehow is almost off the radar in the mass of crime and news that goes on in London. It was a big thing for a day or two locally, but after that, it melted away again.

When you look at it, it's one of those crimes that really gets under your skin because of the pointlessness of it, the unfairness of it.

You've got these two people who have devoted their lives to helping others, carry on like that with their neighbours, then you've got a man whose mind is disturbed and who's abusing substances and becomes paranoid and attacks them. While they should have been looking forward to their twilight years together after this wonderful life they'd had, Maurice had that taken away from him. He was of course injured himself, and fortunate to make a recovery. It's one of those cases that makes you feel quite uncomfortable when you think about it.

They'd taken him under their wing, realising he needed help, and that's the sort of people they were. He called them mum and dad, they treated his children like their own grandchildren and yet he was so paranoid about life really, through drink and drug misuse, that he believed the Baldocks were plotting against him to take his daughter away from him. That unusual combination of circumstances was sufficient to drive him to try to kill them.

You've actually got a man who's got problems with his mental state, difficulties in his life with his child and then you've got a couple who didn't know him, saw he was distressed and not only helped him there and then but continued to help him and show him kindness and support for years afterwards and he pays that back by going into their house and stabbing them while they slept in their bed.

CHAPTER 11
THE MURDER OF KRYSTAL HART

There are a few different kinds of murder case. There's the open and shut case – where somebody is arrested there and then and in custody. Maybe they've been arrested by local police because there's been a fight, they've been nicked at the time and then someone's died. They're pretty basic, and pretty easy to do in many ways.

The ones that were more difficult, I guess, fall into two broad categories - you've got the whodunit and the manhunt. The whodunits were the more interesting and the more fulfilling to do; there was a greater sense of pride or satisfaction in a whodunit maybe. With a manhunt, you know who did it, but you can't find them. The Krystal Hart case is a classic example of the manhunt.

We saw him with the gun in his hand, we heard the shots and we saw him leave with the gun in his hand. It was just a question of finding him. It literally was a manhunt. There was no doubt from the beginning that that was who was responsible for killing and it was just a question of finding him. It requires different skills and different techniques and presents different issues and different problems. On balance I guess I prefer a whodunit to a manhunt.

The murder of Krystal Hart came to us at Easter 2007. It was Good Friday, and we were on call in the office in Putney. There was a skeleton staff on duty, because it was a bank holiday, and it was a fine glorious early April day.

We were working out of Putney at the time and were preparing the case for the Levi Bellfield murders to go to court. My team was back down to a normal size while we were working on that, but we still had to fulfil our obligations of being on call one week in eight and taking the occasional new investigation when we could. It was kind of patting your head and rubbing your stomach at the same time in some ways, because we were still investigating these very serious cases that were part of the Levi Bellfield trial, but we still had to do other cases as well, so we were on call. How it typically worked is that, because you did on call every eight weeks, you tried to get all your jobs solved and charged within six weeks, and then you'd have a week to tidy it up a bit and you'd still have people doing work on it and getting it ready for court.

Battersea wasn't actually in our area, it was South area but they were busy with other things and their on-call team was already deployed. We were in Putney, so we were actually physically based in the South area, although we were actually a West team.

Unusually at 10 or so in the morning – most call-outs tend to be after 5pm in the evening – we got a phone call saying: "We need you to deploy to a shooting in Battersea, the South area, because there's a 22-year-old girl who's been shot dead on her doorstep."

"Yeah ok, any more information?" I replied.

"The victim was called Krystal Hart."

My first question to them was simple: "Do we know if it's a gang-related case?"

The answer came back: "No, we think it's definitely not gang-related, it is more to do with a neighbour dispute."

It was intriguing answer. When people fall out with their neighbours, it's very rarely settled by a shooting. You might have a fight and damage caused and police get called but I had never come across this before, where it had escalated and was resolved by someone shooting someone

We didn't have a whole team at Putney, we had a minimum strength skeleton staff, so I took the officers I had with me. One of them was Jo Brunt, who was still doing case work for Levi Bellfield. She was someone I relied upon for the Levi case and I was glad she was available to come with me. When we got to the scene, Belleville Road in Battersea, we were met by the local DI who was a man called John McFarlane. Up until a few months ago, he'd been on my murder squad, so we knew who we were talking to and he had recent experience. It was nice to know the scene management before we got there was going to be good and the right things had been done. This was the case more often than not; when I used to turn up at callouts to suspicious deaths, I'd often bring the cordon in, people from the borough seem to err on the side of caution when it comes to evidence which is great, very professional. There's an old saying that the Met Police are good at the big things and it's the little things that let them down, but my experience is that when it came to things such as dealing with suspicious deaths they were very capable.

Belleville Road is in this safe, nice part of London, an up-and-coming area with lots of young professionals and families. There were so many nannies and au pairs pushing their charges about the streets there on Wandsworth Common, that the area was known as "Nappy Valley", possibly one of the last places you'd think any murder would take place in London.

When we turn out to a new inquiry, it's always tinged with sadness, because we always know somebody has lost their life. But when we found out the circumstances surrounding Krystal's murder, it was immediately apparent what a real, absolute tragedy and senseless waste of life this one was. It was just the sort of tragedy that even experienced murder squad detectives like my team were shocked by.

Krystal Hart was born and grew up in Battersea, in south west London. She was part of quite a large extended family, and it was, in many ways, a traditional London family with people always supporting each other, they were very close. She had been working as a secretary, in fact she had been working at the office of the then Deputy Prime Minister, John Prescott.

Krystal had been shot in a residential street, at a nice semi-detached house that had been converted to two flats. Krystal occupied the upstairs and used the original front door to the house, there was a kind of a bay window on the front of house and another front door had been put into the side of that bay; it was at a right angle to the original front door and it led to the downstairs flat.

Angie Brewer lived in the flat downstairs to Krystal's, so in the same building but she had the ground floor of the house. Angie was considerably older than Krystal, probably 25-30 years older and she'd had a life with episodes of addiction and difficulties with her mental health. I think it was fair to say that she wasn't a model neighbour and that she would complain about virtually anything that didn't fit in with how she wanted things to be. It could be where the rubbish bags were put, or the noise, anything like that and she would complain not only to the housing association but also to the local police. The local neighbourhood police team knew Angie Brewer very well.

The story was that there had been a history of disputes and friction between Krystal and Angie Brewer, it was the normal low level of arguments between neighbours about silly things; nothing on the face of it that you'd think would make it escalate to a shooting and to murder. The local police had been called a few times and there were a few intelligence reports from the local community officers, as well as a few civil proceedings in the county court to get injunctions or restraining orders to try to resolve it.

It still didn't seem to explain the severity of what happened, Angie Brewer downstairs was reviled by Krystal's family, they hated her and blamed her for all the problems that were occurring there, but Angie Brewer had made a decision in this circumstance after this incident that she was going to assist the police and tell us whatever she could about what went on.

She was the first person to give us an account of the events that morning and she told us that she had a friend called Thomas Hughes who lived less than a mile away. He used to come around and bring things to her and she said herself that he wasn't her boyfriend, but he had a soft spot for her and probably would have liked to have been her boyfriend.

Thomas Hughes was in many ways a sad character. He was another local – his family owned a house less than half a mile from where Krystal lived, through three generations, since it was built in Victorian times. He lived there with his mother, old and infirm, although he was in his 40s.

I think I described him as a wannabe gangster and I think that's pretty accurate – he dabbled in drugs, soft drugs like cannabis, selling some every now and then. He liked people to think he was well-connected and that he was more important in that kind of world than he really was.

Angie Brewer and Thomas Hughes had a connection in their kind of lifestyle, neither had a job, they had a lot of time on their hands, two people who'd drifted together and had common interests – mainly drinking – and they got on. But it was a very uneven partnership because I think Thomas Hughes wanted it to be a formal relationship, while Angie Brewer just saw him as the friend who came round to smoke and drink sometimes.

He'd no doubt heard chapter and verse from Angie Brewer about what an awful neighbour Krystal was and he decided the way to get into her good books, to impress her, was to deal with it.

And while it came as a shock to many that he actually had a firearm, it's probably even more surprising that he went and used the gun. And that he went and used it to shoot and kill Krystal Hart.

Earlier that Good Friday morning, Angie Brewer told us, Hughes had visited her. He'd knocked on her door at about 9 o'clock and brought her an Easter egg. While he was visiting, he'd seen David, Krystal Hart's boyfriend/partner. He didn't live with her, but some words had been exchanged between Hughes and David about parking the cars or the car being in the way. Angie Brewer said that Thomas Hughes had gone away then come back half hour later. She heard him banging on the door that led upstairs to Krystal's flat. He'd made so much noise that Angie Brewer came to her door too and opened it to listen to what was going on. She heard Krystal come downstairs and open the front door, there were just a few words and the next thing she heard was gunshots – a couple of gunshots. She looked out and saw Thomas Hughes walking away with a revolver in his hand, getting into his VW Golf and driving away.

At that point we've got pretty good first hand evidence of exactly what had happened. It was to get better because what we didn't know, and I don't think Angie Brewer knew, was that Krystal Hart, high in her porchway, had installed a CCTV camera on the advice of her lawyers because of the ongoing dispute. The camera was running and it recorded video and sound.

Krystal's family, her mother and aunt, lived nearby and we went around to see them at their flat. Her mother was obviously completely distraught about things, but the family were able to give us an awful lot of the background about what had been going on with Angie Brewer. It kind of added a dimension to the whole case. It was during that meeting, the initial meeting with Krystal's family, that we were given the bombshell: Krystal had been four months pregnant.

We went from there back to the offices in Putney and when we viewed the CCTV, it became clear – this was an unusual investigation, but it was one where we know exactly what happened and we knew exactly who did it. The recording from that morning confirmed almost exactly what Angie Brewer was telling us – we saw the visit by Thomas Hughes, bringing her the Easter egg, we saw him leave, we saw him come back, we saw him with the gun in his hands, we heard the shots, and he left with the gun in his hand. Because he had stepped over Krystal's threshold to shoot her he was off-camera when he pulled the trigger – but we had the soundtrack.

We knew exactly what happened and exactly who did it. We knew what his name was, what his car registration was, what his mobile phone number was. Angie Brewer had given us all of this because she had little choice. Now it was just a question of finding him, it was literally a manhunt.

The post-mortem examination was at St George's mortuary in Tooting, South London. It was pretty much an open and shut case, the death was by gunshot wound. Krystal had been shot twice. She had been shot once in the neck or upper chest area and had gone down; she was then shot in the head while she was on the floor.

It was tantamount to an execution; the second shot aimed at the head was something to make sure that she was dead. We would have to focus our efforts on finding Thomas Hughes because he was out there somewhere with a gun and had just killed someone.

There wasn't much news going on that weekend – it was Easter after all – and the terrible, outrageous nature of the offence meant there was quite a lot of media interest in Krystal's shooting.

The mainstay of our efforts was always going to be to find him through his mobile phone. We quickly got the authority for his service provider to give us live updates on where the phone triangulated and on which masts. I knew the intelligence people would get a trace up on his phone and we could mount that part of the operation very quickly.

We then had Hughes' home address to search, we went down to Stonells Road, just round the corner, he lived that close. It was a funny little street – less than a dozen houses that were all terraced. On the other side of the road was just a wall to a school. We later found out that Thomas Hughes' grandfather built this road and it was named after him. He'd retained one of the houses in the middle for his own use and it became the family home.

It had been left down the line to Thomas' mother who lived there. And it was collapsing.

Every other house down the street had been extensively modernised with loft conversions and basements, it's a prime area for doing things like that in solid Victorian houses. But Hughes' house was the exception, it looked like it had no maintenance, let alone modernisation, for decades.

When we went in, we looked at it and the house was literally falling down. There were cracks in the brickwork, there were window panes askew because the brickwork was sagging. The only person in was Hughes' mother who was quite aged and infirm, as well as a lot of cats. There was a lot of mess, she was living in absolute squalor and he clearly didn't care for her.

We were genuinely frightened it was going to fall down while we were searching it. It was the only time in my career that I had to hold off a search waiting for builders to come with supports for the ceiling and walls, to make the structure safe for police officers to enter. Even then it was advised that I get the smallest, lightest officers to go upstairs to search because they weren't sure what might happen if a heavier officer went in. I certainly stayed downstairs.

The search took place and there was nothing of note, it was obvious that it was the place Thomas Hughes lived. There was a backyard, not so much of a garden, and there, behind a loose brick, was a quantity of ammunition, some of it live and some blank. On the face of it, it looked like it was the same sort of ammunition that came from the gun that killed Krystal. But there was no gun there. Thomas Hughes was still missing, the gun was still missing.

And now we had a second person we had to find accommodation for, as there was no way we could leave his mother without help. We were already helping Angie Brewer find somewhere else to live, and we had to get social services out again. It's not very often on a murder investigation you have to do this soft-skill police work of helping people carry on with their lives and liaise with other agencies, but we had to do it twice in this case which was out of the ordinary.

These hard-nosed murder squad detectives were still police officers and they'd still got this very human side to them. We went in there and found this poor old lady who was completely bewildered. She wasn't in the best of mental health and her son was meant to be looking after her but she was living in absolute abject squalor. There were two tins of tinned stew or something in the house, the only food on the premises. And they were trying to persuade her that she ought to let us take her somewhere where she could be looked after. That was hard enough, but after that there was the equally hard task of trying to find somewhere willing to take her and look after her. It's the kind of thing that our colleagues in uniform do all the time, but for the murder squad to be doing it was slightly unusual.

Jo and I went back to Putney to meet the rest of the team to discuss what we ought to be doing. The kind of forensic work at the scene and the ordinary stuff was taking place, but the focus and the priority was very much to find this man. It wasn't going to be difficult to prove the murder, because we had pictures and sound of him doing it. But, it was just finding him and protecting the public from a gunman who had just killed somebody and was still armed. It's a funny sort of business, chasing somebody who you know has got a gun and has killed somebody and you haven't got a gun.

Myself and Jo Brunt and the other members of the team who were hurtling around south London, trying to find this man, were armed with a stick and some CS spray, that's all. It's one of those strange quirks of how police authority works – you have to have safeguards in place and you need to have a plan when dealing with an armed suspect. Looking for a man who committed a murder with a gun in itself isn't sufficient justification to have an armed response officer. It was difficult to know how we would get armed assistance, it was really one of those cases where we had to suck it and see, try to find where he was and then make a decision on how we approach him to take him into custody. But we couldn't be armed or have armed officers with us on the search for him.

The intelligence DS Clive Grace liaised with the mobile phone companies and we got a trace on the location of Thomas Hughes' phone. But the best a phone company could get – even in these cases where you've got a life at risk and a dangerous person on the streets – was telling us where his phone was every five minutes, or 10 minutes ago. We were playing catch up. We had to hope he stayed somewhere long enough for us to get to that location. We hadn't recovered his car, a black Mark 2 VW Golf, but there weren't that many about and it would be easy to spot in the right area.

The plan was simple – go out looking for him. There was still no trace, but on the first evening there was a succession of pieces of information coming from the mobile phone company via Clive Grace, giving us a location. We'd all rush off and converge on it from different routes, only to be told he'd moved somewhere else. This happened virtually for the rest of that night, even once we got towards midnight there was a suggestion that his phone was at Gatwick, so we thought he was trying to get a flight and leave the country. We all rushed down to Gatwick, only to be told no, he was back at Epsom.

He moved about a great deal the rest of that day into the early hours of Saturday morning, eventually stabilising and staying overnight in the Hook area, between Chessington and Hook. There were people who had been working now for 16-17 hours nonstop on this, myself included. Most of us would have liked to get some sleep at some time because we knew we were going to be busy tomorrow as well. It was imperative to find this man and find this gun. It was going to be all hands to the pumps.

It got to probably 5am and we were satisfied that we had driven up and down every single street, car park and piece of land where that VW Golf could have been parked. We couldn't find it. So, at that point in time we had to call it a day. Then it was literally a couple of hours sleep and back the next morning to carry on.

It wasn't so much sleep as a quick nap, shower and change and we were back out again. The next day was the Saturday, another bright and sunny day. We had found out through some more excellent intelligence work that Thomas Hughes had a boat – a small motor boat – that was moored on the River Thames, somewhere near Richmond. It seemed a little bit odd in some ways because there are some boats there that are pretty expensive, as would be the mooring. We thought it was out of Thomas Hughes' league, but when we got there and found it, we discovered it was just a small dinghy with an outboard motor and canvas cover on top.

By lunchtime on Saturday, it was time to enlist the help of the public and use their eyes and ears. It was time to go public with his name and car details – let's try and enlist the help of millions of Londoners to look for this car and this man. It was quite an unusual step. You have to get authority from a senior officer – releasing a man's name, picture and details of his car, and explaining what he's wanted for, isn't done very often by the police. In this case, I thought it was justified because there was still a real risk that Thomas Hughes was in possession of a real gun and ammunition. He could easily present a danger to members of the public. Fortunately the Deputy Assistant Commissioner agreed with me and gave his authority.

We appeared on lunchtime local news in London and within a half hour of that going out, we had a phone call from somebody, not a million miles away from the scene. still in Battersea, who said: "That black Golf has been outside my fence at my house, and it's been there for the last couple of days."

It looked like Hughes had dumped the car there and then used the train, there was a nearby rail station. All the time his phone had been moving around, we had been looking for the black Golf, but he'd been on public transport. So, we would never have found him through the car.

And then we got a call from Battersea police station. They said: "You know this man Thomas Hughes that you want? Well he just walked into the police station and surrendered."

He'd walked in and said: "I understand the police want to speak to me?"

I asked if he was in custody. "Well, not exactly, no," they replied. He came in, he'd said that he was Thomas Hughes, they'd looked him up and realised he could be armed and dangerous. They asked him to sit in the front office and wait for an armed response vehicle to come. He didn't know that, but they were waiting for their armed colleagues to come and arrest him.

I suppose it was one way of dealing with the risk, it wasn't what I would have done, but everything turned out OK. He played the game and waited there in the front office, the armed response vehicle turned up, he was arrested and delivered to us.

Although we took his clothes and submitted them for analysis, they didn't give us any evidence, but we didn't need it. We had this film which was all the evidence we really needed. He was interviewed and like most people being investigated for serious offences, he was advised not to give any comment to anything that was put to him. He'd just repeat, monotonously, "no comment".

We never did recover the gun and he never told us what he had done with it. As far as he was concerned, he didn't have one, despite the fact that we had found suitable ammunition for it at his house. He gave no explanation for what he had done. He didn't come up with any defence of any sort of what he might have done and why we had the wrong man.

It wasn't really until we came to trial at the Old Bailey that we found out what Thomas Hughes' defence might be. And basically at the trial, it was simply "it wasn't me". It was a strange defence in some ways because we had very good, very clear CCTV footage that showed that it was him. It was merely a matter of putting that footage before a jury, having expert evidence to show the footage as accurate and complete and so forth and it was absolutely plain. You could just look at the pictures and know that was the man. It was no surprise he was convicted of murdering Krystal Hart.

There were many aggravating features to this murder, not least of which she was pregnant and he took the life of that unborn child as well and that he had used a firearm to do it.

When sentencing him, the judge said this was to all intents and purposes a ruthless execution and a truly evil act. He said Hughes would have to serve at least 30 years of his life sentence before he could even apply for parole, which makes him something like 70 years old before he's even got a chance of being out of prison.

It's quite interesting, just another curious thing is that Hughes case came to court not very long – just a matter of a week or two – after Levi Bellfield was sentenced to three whole life terms in my other case.

Strangely enough they formed a bit of a friendship, so much so that Bellfield was heard talking on the phone from prison to his brother about "his mate Tom" and how terrible it was that he got 30 years for this crime.

Certainly, from what I've heard from his conversations with Levi Bellfield in prison, I get the impression that Thomas Hughes feels hard done by and that his sentence was too severe. My view is that he was extremely lucky to get away with just 30 years.

He was an insignificant, rather weedy, scruffy individual who'd just taken someone's life for no reason, so it's hard to think of him as anything other than that.

CCTV technology during the Cullens robbery and Christopher Donovan murder was more primitive, but by the Krystal Hart case it had improved vastly and we were using elements such as mobile phone triangulation. Technology has without doubt helped the police in murder cases. This is often because most murders aren't planned. They come as a result of an argument or something, or another crime going wrong. Very few people leave their house and go out thinking: “I'm going to go and kill someone.” Most murderers haven't thought about technology and the technical things we can do with CCTV, mobile phone data, automatic number plate recognition and all those advancements.

But as it moves on and people know what `they're up against in technological terms, then they can take measures to try and minimise the risk of being caught. That might only happen in one, two, three per cent of all murder cases, but they are the really difficult ones. But I do fear that our reliance upon technology and DNA has, to a degree, de-skilled investigators. Because everybody expects there to be DNA. And you've got to the stage where lawyers expect DNA evidence. the CPS expect DNA evidence so they can try and charge people and even jurors expect DNA evidence because they've all watched Dexter, Silent Witness, Waking The Dead and all those other TV programmes.

If you've got somebody who's bright enough, prepared enough and good enough with their planning to say “I'm going to avoid all these ways of being caught”, then are we getting to the point where there is a danger that our reliance on technology and science will hinder investigations?

DNA has been mainstream now for nearly 30 years, so almost all our police officers have only known a world where DNA exists. If they actually have to do the knocking on doors and gathering bits of circumstantial evidence like my team did for me in the Bellfield case, are they up to it? Have they got the experience of doing it? Can they still do it?

I think it's really an issue for law enforcement generally, but police in particular, to make sure that those sorts of investigative skills are still developed and people still have experience with them. If we just rely on technology to solve crimes, then we're going to be failing even more to solve them.

And because policing has become more results oriented, and because of press interest, I always question the kind of received wisdom that the most recent case is always the most important. If you do that, particularly when things were busy – there was one year I think we got up to 180 murders in London in a year – you have to drop what you're doing and take on another case. And I understand that because of the "golden 48 hours", you have to do the work at the start; it's your best chance of getting something. But what nobody was prepared to do was after a week, say: "Do you know what, this is a no hope case, but we should go back to that one where we had a bit of a chance." That doesn't always happen.

I think the expectations upon, the scrutiny of and desire for accountability of police these days, is huge.

Today's officers police in an environment the likes of which we've never seen before in terms of scrutiny. A lot of it is unofficial scrutiny, with social media and citizen journalism – everybody's got a camera in their pocket. And there's also been scrutiny of police relationships with the media. After that police forces to a large degree withdrew from contact with the media – I said at the time, and I think it's been borne out, that we are nurturing a generation of journalists whose default position now is to criticise the police.

There has been a breakdown in the symbiotic relationship that lasted for decades between police and journalists. Police now don't engage and don't talk to them, or if they do it's all very official. The media can't have blank spaces in their newspapers or dead air in their TV reports, so they look to other sources for that. And those sources may not be as good.

There's certainly no possibility for police to influence those sources. And they tend to come from a position of criticism, first of all, and the police are very, very bad at rebutting it or getting ahead of the curve and communicating what's really going on.

In terms of major crime and how major crime is reported and communicated by the media, there has been a real sea change. It came after Bellfield – on that case I had 28 separate meetings, all documented – with crime reporters from Fleet Street and from the broadcast media. I sat down and explained what the issues in the case were and what we were trying to do and how we were trying to do it. As a senior journalist told me: "Our newsrooms are so much smaller than they used to be, people haven't got time to go out chasing stories."

He said: "If you give them a steer, then you have an influence." That's not saying you can control a story – nobody necessarily wants that – but you could influence it. With Bellfield, we were able to influence the reporting around how bad he was and what a bloody brilliant investigation it was by my team and steer away from the skeletons that were in the cupboard, where things had happened in the past with other people that could have been done better.

CHAPTER 12
THE DISAPPEARANCE OF MAUREEN HALE

In 2008, we were still working on the Levi Bellfield case, so we worked on other cases simultaneously. We were very busy, but I relished it.

My then wife Louise was very understanding, because she's got a background in policing of various sorts. She was not only extremely supportive but she was also very useful, because she had a perspective on things from a slightly different standpoint. I tapped into that. The work did mean long hours and a lot of time at work, but she understood that completely. Did I always manage to make family events and did I always manage to make the kids' birthdays and stuff like that? No, but that was part of being an SIO anyway. It was like that before Bellfield, when I did the Christopher Donovan case, we cancelled a week's holiday because of it.

I'm not one of these people who says my career took precedence, ruined things and made my home life miserable or whatever. It didn't. I think I was probably a much, much better and nicer person to be around when I was busy and when I felt engaged and exercised by what I did at work. I was certainly better to be around compared with the rare, short periods when I was bored and fed up with being at work.

Every SIO and every murder squad in London carries a number of unsolved investigations and sometimes you get the opportunity to move them on when new evidence or something turns up which means it's worthwhile re-opening one of these unresolved cases. There are many justifications for re-opening a stalled case. Quite often it's when advances in science mean you can get DNA from an exhibit you could not get at the time, or perhaps if another witness comes forward.

In the case of the disappearance of Maureen Hale, it was a slightly more unusual circumstance – it was a change in the law.

The double jeopardy rule meant that if you were tried and acquitted, you couldn't be put on trial for the same charge again. The fear for the Maureen Hale case was that if her husband Martin were charged with murder and acquitted – even though her body had never been found – at some point in the future, the body might be discovered and there might be good scientific evidence on that body which would point to his guilt. But under the old law it wouldn't then have been possible to take him to court again. For this reason the chance had never been taken.

When we looked at the circumstances and we were able to lay it out and think about what happened to Maureen Hale, it became an amazingly compelling case and really it appeared, even at my first review, that we didn't need any more evidence than what had been discovered before. But we did find some.

To make some progress with Maureen Hale's disappearance, I gave the case to another part of the team and it was principally, DS Kevin McSharry and DI Andy Perrot who looked at it. Once we were able finally to disentangle ourselves from the Bellfield investigation, then Maureen Hale's disappearance became a priority focus for the team.

I hadn't worked with Kevin McSharry before but he had been around the CID in south west London for a very long time and a lot of people on the team had worked with him; when he became available they encouraged me to try and get him onto our team. I had not a single second of regret that I did so; he was a very capable man. He could be trusted to do everything to a high standard and he did it all with a smile. He's a nice fellow too, a really valuable addition to the team at the time.

Maureen Hale was born as Maureen Weatherly and she got married young; at 19 she wed a man named Agg, and so became Maureen Agg. They soon had a son named Nathan. When that marriage broke down and they parted she took Nathan, who was still quite young, with her and when she got together with Martin Hale, Nathan was adopted into their new family. Although they went on to have four more children, Nathan was very much part of the family and they always thought of themselves as a family of seven.

Maureen Hale really fell nicely into her role as sort of stockbroker-belt mother – she didn't work, she didn't have to work, Martin's wholesale greengrocery business was booming. She spent her time looking after the children and then, while the children were at school, it would be coffee mornings and gym sessions and socialising with the other women in the area that were in a similar position to her. She had a lot of friends and to all external appearances she had an idyllic life.

Martin Hale was essentially a self-made man. He started off on a fruit and vegetables stall at Kingston Market and by the 1990s he had built up a business worth over a million pounds, based at Western International Market in Hounslow. It was wholesaling fruit and vegetables and was a very lucrative business for him. He employed two or three people and the profits from the company meant they could afford to live in Ember Court Road, in a five-bedroom detached house in the Surrey stockbroker belt.

But the job did have its pressures for Hale, it was a trade that operates exclusively in the first half of the day. It meant that for years he was getting up at two in the morning six days a week and although he was home by lunchtime, that sort of lifestyle would put pressure on anybody. He would come home, grab some sleep and then be back again early hours of the morning. It had great rewards, but it was a tough life.

All this took a toll on their marriage and they started arguing. And Maureen, despite all the wonderful surroundings she had, the house and the children and the lifestyle, thought there must be more to life than this. She began thinking about being with somebody else and that was what led her into starting affairs outside their marriage.

Unhappy and feeling she wasn't getting the companionship she wanted from Martin, the first person

Maureen turned to was a man called John Potter, a local plumber who did work for them at their home. It didn't work out for her – they went out for a drink and they'd had a quick kiss in the car. But for some reason Martin suspected something was going on between the two and had put a recording device in Maureen's car. He got a recording of her with Potter, confronted her with it, she owned up and it caused further conflict between them.

It's perhaps worth remarking that most people don't feel the need to put listening devices into their partner's cars. There was obviously something going on that put some sort of suspicion in Martin Hale's mind that Maureen might be up to something, or else he wouldn't have gone to those lengths.

Clearly Martin Hale had a lot to lose, if Maureen walked out the door and divorced him, there were five children, there was an expensive house and a thriving business, she would have had claims on all of those.

The next time Maureen was more careful. She struck up a relationship with a man called Andrew Horton, a gardener who worked at the military cemetery at Brookwood. Maureen Hale had been visiting with friends to look at the gardens and grounds, got into a conversation with him and they exchanged phone numbers. It's quite fair to say Andrew Horton was someone you'd describe as a ladies' man, he would regularly attempt to make new relationships with women he encountered during his job, with frequent successes. Maureen, although she was absolutely devoted to her children, had become disillusioned with the marriage and there were one or two episodes of severe arguing between her and Martin, and even some domestic violence although she suffered no serious injuries. Maureen decided in 1999 that the marriage wasn't going anywhere; she needed to be out of it and filed for divorce.

This all came to a head on June 22 1999, the very day that Maureen had divorce papers served on Martin Hale. At about 10pm that night they had a terrible row, it was a blazing, noisy row that all the children heard. Martin Hale's version of events was that at the end of that argument, Maureen took up, left the house and was never to be seen again.

Some three days after Maureen Hale had disappeared – June 25 – her husband Martin Hale went to Kingston Police Station to report her missing. The missing person report, as they all are, was assessed by supervising officers to see if anything else needed to be done. Finally in the middle of July, two to three weeks after the report was made, police in Kingston decided to arrest Martin on suspicion of murder. They didn't have the evidence to charge him unless he admitted it once he was arrested. But it did give them the opportunity to interview him, get his side of the story, his account and also to search both his home and his workplace.

If Martin Hale were to be believed and Maureen had just upped and left after the argument, she did so without any basic necessities – no clothing, no means of support, no money, no means of communication and no transport. No trace of Maureen Hale existed officially after that moment. She hadn't spoken to her doctor or dentist, hadn't used her bank account or phone. Everything was just dead. There was no trace of her in any way. She hadn't contacted any of her friends or family and, crucially, she hadn't contacted any one of her five children. Everyone said that was completely out of character, even if it had all got too much for her and she had deliberately disappeared, she would undoubtedly have maintained contact with those children.

There were several things that were out of the ordinary in relation to Martin Hale's business on the night Maureen went missing. First, he called his manager and told him he was unwell and wouldn't be in at work that night. But the manager drove past Martin Hale's house at 2am – as he did every day as they used to check each other to make sure they'd woken up – and he noticed Martin's BMW car was missing. He found this a bit odd; his boss had phoned him and said: "I'm not well, I'm not coming to work." But when he went past the house in the early hours of the morning the car wasn't there, which implied Martin was out, elsewhere.

When the manager got to work he found there was a spade missing, a tool they used every day for clearing up bits of rubbish and old fruit and veg. They had to find another way of doing it for a few days and then Martin Hale brought the spade back to work and no one asked him about it – he was the boss, he could do what he liked. But it was an odd thing that he would want to use the spade at home in that period after Maureen had gone missing.

Lastly, both Martin Hale as the owner of his business and his manager had company cars but they were very different, Martin's was a 7 Series BMW whereas the manager had a little Ford Fiesta, yet Martin had swapped the cars after Maureen disappeared, trading down.

"Well I just fancied a change, I'm allowed to change my mind, they are both cars belonging to my business and I'm entitled to drive them," he said, "and I just fancied driving something different for a while."

In his briefcase were the divorce papers Maureen had sent to him but also with them was a pad and on that pad, in Martin Hale's own handwriting, there was a numbered list of four choices, which he admitted to writing. "At sea, landfill, by acid, by fire," it said. When he was asked why he had written that he said: "I've been having some dark thoughts." He admitted that he was thinking of killing his wife and how he would dispose of her body. He had written that down as his brainstorming session with himself, but he said he wouldn't have gone through with it.

"Yes, I did write it," he said, "that's what they are, I was in a particularly dark place, but it doesn't mean that I did it, I was just writing down dark thoughts."

When the double jeopardy rule was changed and it became possible to try people twice for the same murder, that removed the barrier to prosecuting him,. So in 2008 we decided to re-open the investigation thinking that, even if we couldn't find the body, we still had a chance of a conviction.

When we started to resume the investigation of Maureen Hale's disappearance, the first thing we did was repeat all those enquiries that had been made nearly a decade before when she went missing. We looked at her bank account and at her GP, dentist and hospital records; we spoke to all her friends and family we could trace and we got the same answers: nothing. There was still no trace of her, she had had no brush with officialdom since 1999.

We then set about searching for her body. It is so difficult to search in that part of the world; there are so many woods and forests and open spaces. We'd seen that in the Millie Dowler investigation, where Surrey police searched their county virtually continually for six months and still never completed it. There was no way we could conceive a speculative search like that. The cost of open space searches is astronomical so if we were to embark upon such an activity it would need to be based on firm intelligence, with a perception there was a good chance of success.

When it came to the searches for Maureen Hale's body, we had to be selective. The only place that we had any source of intelligence or idea that it was a good place to look was the family home. They had a large garden and we searched not only inside the house and the whole building but the entire grounds. We even went so far as to remove a recently-erected shed and looking beneath it. We had ground penetrating radar there to see if areas of land had been disturbed and the whole thing took four days. It was quite a large operation and of course it came to nothing and we found no trace of her there.

There was another remarkable piece of evidence discovered. Martin Hale had a habit of drinking at a sports club that was effectively in the middle of Sandown Park racecourse, there was a bar and he used to go in there and drink. We discovered that just a day or two after Maureen went missing he had been at the bar and had there met a man he went to school with and whom he hadn't seen in 30 or 40 years.

He chatted to him and the man told him that he was working as the general manager of a pet cemetery and golf course in Cobham called Silvermere. Martin said: "That sounds interesting I might pop down and have a look." The man he was speaking to thought that Martin meant the golf course; that he wanted to play golf, but when Martin turned up the very next day, it wasn't the golf course he was interested in – it was the crematorium. He asked the manager if he ever rented out the incinerators at the crematorium. The owner looked at him aghast. "No," he replied. Martin Hale then said: "What if I were to offer you £20,000, would you let me borrow one for the weekend then?"

I thought this a staggering piece of evidence, his wife had gone missing two days before and there he was offering a large sum of money to use an incinerator at a crematorium,. Given that, realistically, the only use for one of those is to dispose of a body. He later told us: "No, that didn't happen, I went there, I spoke to the man in charge, who was an old friend from primary school, but I went there to look and talk about the golf course, not about the pet crematorium."

The legal position is when someone has gone missing and there is no proof of life for more than seven years you can apply to court to have them deemed dead. It leaves you free to marry again and also claim on any insurance policy in existence. The person is legally treated as dead then, even though there is no hard evidence of it. As we understood it, very shortly after that seven-year period was up, Martin Hale made the application to the court and the court had no option but to declare her dead – there was absolutely no trace of her being alive since that day in 1999 when she was last seen.

Our thinking was clear: "If you put everything we know about this case to the jury, you have Hale trying to lose his car for a few days, borrowing a shovel from work, listing on a piece of paper ways he might dispose of his wife's body, then asking if he could pay a large sum of money to rent a pet crematorium for the afternoon."

There was so much there to build a circumstantial case that I thought it was time we went to the CPS and asked: "What do you think?"

It didn't take the CPS long to come back to us. "Yes, we've looked at this circumstantial evidence and we think there's a realistic prospect of conviction here based on the criteria. Go and charge him."

When Martin Hale was arrested, he was polite, he was a reasonable man, he was a man who ran a business and knew how to interact with people. He was interviewed and he denied knowing anything more than he had said before about the disappearance of his wife, that he had nothing to do with it at all.

We were never able to find Maureen Hale's body but nevertheless we went to court in 2008 and we were reasonably confident that we had enough evidence. We thought any reasonable jury would look at the facts and conclude she must have been murdered by him.

We felt desperately sorry for the Hale children. They didn't know which way to turn, once we'd arrested and charged Martin Hale, because they'd already lost their mother, they'd lived with their father growing up, most of them were adults. It was really difficult for us to deal with them – they wanted to be supportive of their father and we tried to deploy family liaison officers to them as we would do to the children of any murder victim.

But of course, the difficulty was, the suspect was also very close to them. It was a really unusual situation, perhaps even more so because they'd spent the last seven or eight years thinking their mother deserted them and had grown up living only with their father. There were many conflicted ideas and views for those young people to understand. It was something we were never really able to come to terms with satisfactorily. The relationship we had with the children was always a little bit at arm's length, it wasn't like a normal family liaison relationship because of that.

By the time the case came to trial in 2009, Martin Hale had already had his wife, Maureen, declared legally dead by the court, so although we had to go through the process of proving we could find no trace of her being alive, I really don't think that was an issue for the jury, their sole issue was who had killed her.

The defence case was clearly that Martin Hale had nothing to do with it. He couldn't answer for anything he hadn't answered already, and he didn't know what happened to his wife she just left. What they did do was exploit the lover Andrew Horton, who was called as a witness. He gave a rather colourful account of his lifestyle, his philandering and misogyny. He told the jury about how he would often have several lovers on the go at the same time and I don't think he endeared himself to the jury. The defence also called a couple of his former girlfriends; the jury heard how he was violent towards them and he threatened on one occasion to kill one of them.

All that you need is a reasonable doubt and all it needed was a couple of members of that jury to think this rather unsavoury character they saw before them could be responsible for this murder. It was a three-week trial and at the end of the trial Martin Hale was found not guilty and allowed to leave a free man.

I was sitting at Kingston Crown Court waiting for the verdict and it came rather more quickly than we might have expected. And it's a fool's game really to try and read into that because you can have guilty verdicts very quickly and you can have not guilty verdicts very quickly. But given the amount of evidence we had presented to the court, I kind of expected it to take a little bit longer for the jury to deliberate through it.

I was shocked, genuinely shocked, because I thought we had delivered a compelling case. We'd worked hard at it and I thought if the jury accepted the evidence we'd discovered, then they were bound to convict him. It's always difficult when you think you've got a good and solid case, you go to court, and the jury acquit. It had happened countless times during my police career in more trivial cases but this was to be the only murder case I ever lost at court.

We had a mass of circumstantial evidence, all the evidence about Maureen not connecting with officialdom, with her bank, her doctors or anything like that, missing out on important family events, walking out and never saying a word again to her five children. Add to that the fact that on the night she went missing, Martin Hale borrowed a spade he took from his place of work which he didn't take back for a few days. And bizarrely he swapped his 7 Series BMW with his manager's car, a

Ford Fiesta. He didn't swap that back until after he had been arrested by police and they'd searched the Fiesta.

But the fact is, it's the prosecution that bring the case and they have to prove it beyond any reasonable doubt. If any member of the jury has a reasonable doubt they have to say not guilty. And I think the main reason that the jury found a doubt was Andrew Horton. You had the question hanging there, you had Maureen's lover at the time is this man, who has a record of using violence towards women. Is it possible, members of the jury, that he might have killed her?

Ultimately, professionally, I did my job, I got a team together to get the most evidence we could and put it before a court and then the rest of that process takes over. When Martin Hale was arrested by Kevin McSharry and others from my team, he was actually in a car with a Brazilian man and subsequently, after his trial and acquittal, Martin went with this man to Brazil for a period of time. They came back to the UK, both living at the house in Ember Court Road and some of the children were still there.

Of course, during the trial, the fact that Martin Hale might have been in another relationship himself was never put forward to the jury and indeed it was difficult for us to work out, we still don't really know how long this relationship had been going on and whether that was prior to Maureen's disappearance or something that occurred afterwards.

I maintain that the depth and breadth of evidence that we presented to the court in this case exceeded that in many other cases I had where the defendant was found guilty. After Martin Hale's acquittal, the Met Police re-assessed the case and decided not to proceed with the enquiries any further, the case effectively now is closed.

We took every opportunity there was, we found new evidence, we found compelling evidence. The only clincher may have been had we been able to find Maureen's body, because that may have given us more scientific evidence, or its location might have pointed towards her husband's guilt or otherwise.

It's increasingly difficult in the 21st century to disappear without trace. Everything and everybody has a record, phone, money, doctor, dentist, all sorts of things and there was simply no trace of Maureen Hale from the day she was last seen. I'm sure she's dead.

It was the only case I did where we didn't find a body. And it was also the only murder case that I had go to court and the defendant was acquitted. It was very frustrating. It wasn't one I expected us to get to court and lose.

Having not long before convicted Bellfield on wholly circumstantial evidence, it seemed reasonable that we could do it again with wholly circumstantial evidence on this one too. There was a lot of it as well. Some of the things in that case, you look at the evidence and what witnesses were saying and you think, well, if you didn't murder them, why? What was that all about? Why would you do that if not?

It's down to the jury. You only have to have a slight doubt and that's it. That's the way it is and that's the way it should be. You can't get too hung up and disappointed about it. You have to accept that sometimes that's going to happen. It was quite common in policing, even if you had evidence, although less common in murder squads.

It was difficult and I felt for the children, they were in an awful position. They'd lost their mum and we had evidence that the children had to give, that we wanted for the trial. But at the same time, we were doing family liaison with them, working with them, they were the victim's family. It was unusual, to say the least. They'd lost their mum, because she's missing presumed murdered, and faced losing their dad if he were convicted because he'd be in prison.

There's a desire to see the person you thought was the killer found guilty for this crime. But it's also the idea of not knowing – what happened to Maureen Hale? What happened to her body?

If what we think happened actually happened, then it was awful. I think we succeeded in securing a wealth of evidence and we presented it all to the jury and saying: "You decide what you think." I was just very surprised by their conclusion.

EPILOGUE

Levi Bellfield was convicted in February 2008. My retirement date was scheduled for 2011, so I had a bit under three years still to do.

The first six months or so afterwards were a bit of a blur. I was spending a lot of time going and talking to officers and others, doing lectures and talks about it. It was such a major event nationally, the media had imprinted that Bellfield image in the minds of the public. The case was such that a lot of the casework we'd achieved hadn't been done before.

While we were wrapped up in the Bellfield investigation, we had so many other offences to look at and manage, I'd set up a structure whereby I had extra detective inspectors and we kind of split the cases up into little groups that were relevant to each other. We had a DI in charge of those and then a DS was responsible for each individual case. We had this hierarchy that worked – it was the only way I could manage the whole thing.

But what that did was when we came out of the heavy caseload, I had a group of DIs and DSs who had had more exposure and more freedom and more autonomy than they were used to. There was a point when we went back to doing the "ordinary" murders; and by that I mean our case load of shorter and simpler investigations. And they didn't really need me anymore – because they were just that good after getting all this experience.

It took me a little while to get my head around and then it took a particularly tricky case that we got given one day that was difficult, not just in the investigation, but in that it involved a 16-year-old black youth who had been stabbed to death.

It was a big case media-wise as well, so I took an interest in that and it gave me my sense of purpose or my sense of importance or usefulness back again. After I came out of the first meeting about it where I had been more hands on in the briefing, one of the officers just said to me: "Welcome back guv'nor." And I knew what she meant, it was probably the first time for six months I'd really grabbed hold of a meeting and said "this is what we're doing".

That was interesting, then I got asked to do Operation Minstead, and I could have carried on doing that for ages. I may well have stayed beyond the time I had to before my retirement date.

I didn't realise I wasn't going back to the murder squad until about two weeks later when I went back to my office and found that all my stuff was packed up in a box in the corner and somebody was sitting in my desk.

It wasn’t my decision. I never was the greatest “company” man, I didn't really do job politics, meaning, I didn't really do the internal politics of the Metropolitan Police very well. I was always focused on doing what was the task in hand – solving murders. And I think that was something that frightened some people above me.

I think there were two ways of looking at it once we had come out of doing Bellfield. Maybe the powers-that-be thought that we – and me particularly – had got a bit too big for our boots after the case, maybe that. Or they could take the view, that because we've done that, we were so good that we were kind of untouchable.

It didn’t come from my colleagues, not from my peers, the other DCIs, but from some people above – there was a little bit of push back, maybe a sort of reset.

And I think somebody decided that it would probably be easier for someone else to manage the team if I wasn't there. I got edged to one side. I think there was also an element of thinking “not only can we slide him out, but we're going to give him something that's so bloody difficult, he won't be able to succeed”. And that was Minstead, the Night Stalker case.

I was fortunate enough that we did succeed in that too. And in doing so, I got the satisfaction and the thrill of doing something really important, something that was really going to make a difference in terms of saving people, particularly women, from being victimised – just as we had in the Bellfield case. It gave me an opportunity to do that all over again.

I didn't like leaving my team, but they were, in truth, already splitting up a bit then anyway. We had people who’d said they weren’t going to take promotion for a year, or people who'd been selected for promotion and said they were going to take it later, because they wanted to do the Bellfield case. We had people who'd done really well then and wanted to go off and make their own careers.

I never regret the fact that I left that team when I did. I'd been there for six and a half years, by far the longest I'd ever worked in the same place with the same people in my whole service. It was longer than most people work with the same people in their careers. And so, you know, I don't bemoan the fact that I went and as I say, it gave me an opportunity to make a difference with something else. And I was lucky enough that I was able to succeed again.

After Minstead and after Delroy Grant was charged, there was never really any question he'd be convicted. There was DNA evidence. I made noises to see if I could go back to an ordinary murder team. Not necessarily my own old team, but anywhere. And some very senior people in the Met said: "No, you've got to stay with it until it goes to court."

"Well, this won't go to court until after my retirement date," I replied.

"Well, you've got to stay with it."

They had their reasons for thinking that they needed me still there in charge, but for the last 10 months, I was to stay in Lewisham. I won't go into the reasons, but they were explained to me.

I understood, but on a personal level, I was livid. I lived 49 miles away from Lewisham Police Station. I had to drive 49 miles every morning to go in and if there was nothing from the CPS or nothing that really needed my attention, which was most days, I didn't really have anything to do. We had other people getting the case ready for court, that wasn't the SIO's role. I actually got bored.

The only good thing was being on the superintendent's rota to act up as superintendent for murder across London once every six or seven weeks. It was quite a responsibility but it meant that for a whole week you were involved in every suspicious death in the capital. You'd oversee it until it was taken over by a murder squad and you'd decide which squad could take it. You'd make sure they had the resources and all the things they needed.

I had some interesting cases performing that role, most notably Gareth Williams, the intelligence officer found dead in his bathroom, in a holdall, zipped up. One week in every seven I actually felt useful, but the rest of the time was literally just sitting there. With hindsight I wish I had used that time more productively. I could have done the old cold cases that I've been involved in, but it never occurred to me until much later. I wish I had thought about it back then.

It was all a little bit sad. When I finally worked out the dates, I realised I had enough leave owing to me that I thought I would be able to stop work on my 50th birthday, which was in November, and then have enough leave days to go through from Christmas and to my 30-year date, January 4 2011. But I actually ended up just one day short. I stopped working on my birthday, booked all my leave except for one day in December and went over to my best friend's in Austria – he'd just bought a bar in a ski resort. I was there for a couple of weeks to help him get that ready and then had to come back for my one remaining day's duty.

It was December 10 2010 – the day that I went with six of my amazing colleagues from the Bellfield case to Scotland Yard to get our commendations from the then Assistant Commissioner, Cressida Dick. My last day's duty I ever actually did was going with all those wonderful people I'd been through so much with; getting our certificates, shaking hands and going to the pub, which was a brilliant way to bow out really.

The funny thing was I hung onto my warrant card, radio, handcuffs and all the other things you have until the very last day. I went over to Lewisham and there was a young woman in her early 20s who was an assistant in the HR department there; I went in with all my stuff and said my last ever task as a police officer was to give it all to her. She barely looked up, saying: "OK thanks very much." And that was it. That was 30 years, just gone by like that.

I'm not sentimental like that, but it's a bit of a sad way to end it all. It was just a task to her: "Someone's leaving, I've got to take his stuff."

I don't know what I expected. I didn't think there'd be flag-wavers and a brass band – but it would have been nice to have something. Just someone there to say thank you and good luck? It was very anti-climactic, that's the best way to describe it.

I started writing the book about the Bellfield case, but I didn't think it was any good. I had this idea that what that team had done was just so incredible and so worthy of putting into print. There were millions of words and millions of minutes of sound and vision about Bellfield, but nobody had actually written about what the team had done, there was very little about them. Somebody had to do it, because they were just so unbelievably good.

I started writing then, but I didn't really have the confidence. Then I got a job driving a van for a florist shop in Surrey, delivering flowers. It was great fun, people were pleased to see me when I knocked on the door for once. Some of it was like being a PC again – you'd go to an old lady, it would be her birthday and the family sent her flowers. She'd say: "Oh excuse me, while you're here could you just come and get something down in the kitchen for me." Or: "My laptop's not working, could you help?"

It was mad on Mother's Day, Christmas Eve and Valentine's Day. It was like a military operation, or something you'd plan for public order in the police.

I separated from my then wife and moved back north of London to be close to my roots, friends and my family. I knew I was going to do a little bit of TV work because I bumped into a crime producer for ITV and had done a few things on the Bellfield case. I ended up doing some bits for them which was easy as I was living close to London.

When I met my current wife, it meant moving to East Anglia as she had a job there, making it more difficult to get to London. But I also realised there was a point coming where I felt that things were changing so quickly in policing that once you get to four or five years retired, you're not really across all the issues and the difficulties that people have and my insight and experience wasn't as relevant as it once was. I took a back seat and do very little of that sort of punditry now unless it's about Levi Bellfield, who keeps on managing to get himself in the news.

I then started doing documentary work, but it was real boiler room stuff in some ways – I'd be the talking head about cases I knew nothing about. But then I played golf at a charity event and I bumped into Tony Carne from Revelation Films. I was introduced to him, we chatted a bit and I later met with him and his partner at Revelation Trevor Drane to talk about true crime films, how they were made. I had this very fixed view that a lot of true crime was far too focused on the perpetrator and the horror of serious crime, but there were great stories to be told about the investigators and the victims' families. We agreed and that's how The Real Manhunter started.

We wanted to present murder cases in a different way, in a way which was just as interesting but less gory and less celebratory of the perpetrators. It seems to work and I actually think in some respects we've moved the dial in true crime. Other people who make true crime films now talk the talk about doing it that way – I'm not sure they all walk the walk.

It's the way we've done it and has been very successful. We've just finished making the fourth season now so we must be doing something right. And I've enjoyed working with them very much. They know what they're doing, they don't sensationalise and they really get it – they understand what's important to people like me.

I was also put in touch with Ed Whitmore, a screenwriter. He wanted some help with a script he was writing. It was fiction, but he wanted to make it as authentic as possible. We got on like house on fire; he's like a complete encyclopaedia of murder across the world – he's incredible. He gave me some advice on my book and then phoned me one day and said I needed to come to lunch in London with somebody called Philippa Braithwaite. He told me she was Martin Clunes' wife and ran a production company – they make Doc Martin – and she was interested in my book about Levi Bellfield. I hadn't actually completed it then, but the next thing I knew, I had an option from Buffalo for a book I hadn't written yet to turn it into a TV series.

Ed came and stayed with me and we wrote the first episode. Buffalo sent it to ITV and eventually ITV liked it and ordered two more episodes to make it a three-parter. The summer of 2017 was a flurry of typing. Thankfully Ellen was always there to encourage and inspire me to get it done. I had to finish the book too and Ed and I worked together on the script by an extended game of email ping-pong. I'd done a long outline for the whole story and he picked the scenes he wanted for the drama and I then wrote the chapters. We stitched it together in that way.

It sounds like a mad way of doing it, but it actually worked. By the time I saw it, I was used to the idea of Martin Clunes playing me; I thought he did a brilliant job. He's a really talented actor and a lovely guy, so it was great working with him.

Buffalo was great too, not your normal TV production company. The only difficult thing for me was when I was writing the script with Ed, I'd end up talking about myself in the third person. It was just weird. We set out to make the most realistic representation of a murder squad in the 2000s in London that we could and I think we achieved it. Both seasons of Manhunt were a roaring success, each amassing 9 million viewers per episode. The second season even got nominated for the Best Drama BAFTA. And each of my first two books was in the Sunday Times best-sellers top 10 for a couple of weeks too. I'm sure when Miss Jones was teaching me English in the third form at Latymer she never thought that would happen to anything I had written!

I've just been very blessed, lucky even. I was in the right place at the right time. Things have happened to me and I've been riding the wave. I'll keep doing it until nobody wants me anymore. And when I become irrelevant again in a couple of years' time, I'll just go back and play more golf, navigate in more rallies and walk more dogs.

There are so many people who have to work for 40 or 50 years and hate every minute of it. I had 30 years in the police where I loved it and now I'm doing this and I love it again. I've had two careers – and in different ways each has been totally fulfilling but also great fun.

ACKNOWLEDGEMENTS

This book is dedicated to the victims

To their friends, families and loved ones, thank you for allowing us to tell their stories

My additional thanks go out to:

Everyone who has appeared in The Real Manhunter

Everyone who has been involved in producing the series – the production team, crew and creatives

Jack Oliver

Emily-Jayne Wilde

Tim Murray

And of course the wonderful officers I had the privilege of working with, who made me who I am

Printed in Great Britain
by Amazon

62357503R00143